KEY TO Writing

TEACHER'S BOOK 2

CHRISTINE MOORCROFT ♦ LES RAY

Letts

Published by Letts Educational
The Chiswick Centre
414 Chiswick High Road
London W4 5TF
Tel: 020 8996 3333
Fax: 020 8742 8390
E-mail: mail@lettsed.co.uk
Website: www.letts-education.com

Letts Educational is part of the Granada Learning Group. Granada Learning is a division of Granada plc.

© Christine Moorcroft and Les Ray, 2003

First published 2003

ISBN 184085 9385

The authors assert the moral right to be identified as the authors of this work.

All rights reserved. Any educational institution that has purchased one copy of this publication may make duplicate copies for use exclusively within that institution. Permission does not extend to reproduction, storage in a retrieval system, or transmittal, in any form or by any means, electronic, mechanical, photocopying, recording or otherwise, of duplicate copies for loaning, renting or selling to any other institution without the prior permission in writing of the publisher.

British Library Cataloguing in Publication Data
A catalogue record for this book is available from the British Library.

Concept development, design and production for Letts Educational by Start to Finish, 9 Whitecross Square, Cheltenham GL53 7AY

Commissioned by Kate Newport
Project management by Phillipa Allum
Designed and typeset by Paul Manning
Illustrations by Linda Jeffrey, Carol Jonas and Ruth Palmer
Production by PDQ
Printed and bound in Italy by Amilcare Pizzi

Acnowledgement
Crown copyright material is reproduced with the permission of the Controller of HMSO and the Queen's Printer for Scotland.

Contents

Introduction 4

Key to Writing Book 3

Target statements for writing 5

Summary of NLS objectives covered 6

Teacher's notes 8

Photocopiable activity sheets 18

Key to Writing Book 4

Target statements for writing 34

Summary of NLS objectives covered 35

Teacher's notes 38

Photocopiable activity sheets 48

Introduction

Key to Writing teaches children how to improve their writing skills through learning from, and modelling their writing on, the work of experienced writers. The series takes into account the close relationship between reading and writing; the one supports the other. It presents a varied selection of passages from fiction, poetry, drama and non-fiction as appropriate to the recommended range for Years 1 to 6. The passage in each unit suggests the theme, context and purpose for the children's writing and provides a structure to help them to get started. The activities based on the passages develop the children's grammatical and writing skills in a way which helps them to use them in their writing.

Key to Writing is based on the National Literacy *Framework for Teaching* text-level objectives; it also draws on the sentence- and word-level objectives which make a direct contribution to the particular piece of writing.

The Pupil's Books

The activities in each unit of the Pupil's Books are grouped in three sections:

a which focuses on demonstration. It introduces the children to, or extends their experience of, a particular type of text. It encourages them to investigate the text in the passage and consider important features of style

b which focuses on specific aspects of the text which are sometimes linked to the word- and sentence-level objectives relevant to the children's writing. It helps them to understand how writers use grammar and how they choose vocabulary, and makes the consideration of word- and sentence-level skills an integral part of the children's writing. It also encourages the children to use the passage as a model and to write in the style of the passage, using the features they have identified

c which focuses on the children's own writing and is supported by the notes in the relevant **Teacher's Book**. Photocopiable **activity sheets** in the Teacher's Books provide further support for many of the writing activities.

In each unit, from Book 3 onwards, there are suggestions to help the children to improve the presentation of their writing, using ICT where appropriate.

The Teacher's Books

The Teacher's Books provide lesson notes to help teachers to draw out the important features of each passage and to guide pupils so that they can make the transition from writing with support to writing independently. Helping children to make this transition is one of the most difficult aspects of teaching writing. The notes include focused questions and discussion, as well as photocopiable **activity sheets**.

Each set of **teacher's notes** in this book provides guidance on starting the lesson, developing sentence- and word-level skills and points to consider during the plenary session for Pupil's Books 3 and 4:

- **Starting the lesson** includes discussion points which help to introduce the text or draw attention to specific aspects once the children have read it. The children should be encouraged to consider these points in their own writing.
- **Sentence and word level** provides ideas to help the children to use grammar to control their writing and to select words with the meanings they want and which create the effects they intend.
- **Plenary session** concentrates on monitoring and assessment. It provides a focus for the sharing of the children's writing and on constructive criticism of one another's writing. It suggests areas to note which might need further work for individuals or for the class.

Target Statements for Writing

YEAR 3

Phonics and spelling	<ul><li>Attempt to spell unfamiliar words using known conventions and rules and a range and spelling of strategies including phonemic, morphemic and etymological.</li><li>Spell words containing common prefixes and suffixes, e.g. *un-*, *dis-*, *-ly*, *-ful*.</li><li>Spell inflected forms of words containing a short vowel, doubling the final consonant where necessary, e.g *win — winning*, *beg — begged*.</li></ul>	**WORD**
Handwriting	<ul><li>Write legibly with a joined hand, maintaining consistency in size and spacing.</li></ul>	
Style: language effects	<ul><li>Use interesting vocabulary; vary use of adjectives and verbs for impact.</li><li>Select nouns to be specific, e.g. *poodle* rather than *dog*.</li><li>Use terminology appropriate to text type.</li></ul>	**SENTENCE**
Style: sentence construction	<ul><li>Write simple and compound sentences.</li><li>Begin to use some subordinators, e.g. *if*, *so*, *while*, *though*, *since*.</li><li>Vary openings of sentences to avoid repetition.</li></ul>	
Punctuation	<ul><li>Demarcate sentences in the course of writing, using full stops, capital letters, question and exclamation marks, usually accurately.</li><li>Begin to use speech marks and capital letters for a range of purposes.</li><li>Secure the use of commas in a list.</li></ul>	
Purpose and organisation	<ul><li>Use 1st and 3rd person and tense consistently.</li><li>Use a range of connectives which signal time.</li><li>Vary story openings to create effects, such as building tension and suspense, creating moods, establishing character and scene setting.</li><li>Begin to address reader, for instance, by using questions in non-fiction.</li><li>Write narrative with a build-up and with complication which leads towards a defined ending, using a paragraph for each.</li><li>In non-fiction, begin by using basic structure, e.g. introductory and concluding statements in non-chronological reports.</li><li>Sequence sentences to extend ideas logically.</li><li>Use language and structures from different text types for own writing.</li></ul>	**TEXT**
Process	<ul><li>Generate and collect suitable words and phrases before writing.</li><li>Use different planning formats, e.g. charting, mapping, flow charts, simple storyboards.</li><li>Make and use notes.</li><li>Identify and consider audience and how this affects writing.</li><li>Mentally rehearse writing, and cumulatively re-read, making adaptations and corrections.</li><li>Be able to improve own writing and correct errors.</li><li>Use IT to polish and present.</li></ul>	

© Crown copyright 2000

Book 3

Summary of NLS objectives covered in *Key to Writing Book 3*

Unit		Theme	NLS objectives covered
1	Nan's Story	Fiction: Story Ideas	• To generate ideas relevant to a story by brainstorming, word association, and so on.
2	Soccer Shadows	Fiction: Story Talk	• Using reading as a model, to write passages of dialogue.
3	No Problem, Davy	Fiction: Story Places	• To develop the use of settings in their own stories by writing short descriptions of known places and writing a description in the style of a familiar story.
4	Story Openings and Endings	Fiction: Starting and Finishing a Story	• To investigate and collect sentences or phrases for story openings and endings, and to use some of these formal elements in re-telling and story writing.
5	The Hundred-Mile-an-Hour Dog	Fiction: Paragraphs	• To begin to organise stories into paragraphs. • To begin to use paragraphing in the presentation of dialogue in stories.
6	The Story of Persephone	Fiction: What Happened?	• To plan the main points as a structure for story-writing. • To consider how to capture points in a few words which can be elaborated later. • To discuss different methods of planning.
7	Goldilocks	Fiction: Putting It In Order	• To describe and sequence key incidents in a variety of ways, for example: by listing, charting, mapping, making simple storyboards.
8	The Legend of Rama and Sita	Fiction: Story People	• To write portraits of characters, using a story text to describe behaviour and characteristics, and to present portraits in a variety of ways, for example: as posters, labelled diagrams or letters to friends about the characters.
9	The Parable of the Seeds	Fiction: Story Plan	• To write a story plan for their own myth, fable or traditional tale, using a story theme from reading but substituting different characters or changing the setting.
10	The Little Match Girl	Fiction: What If …?	• To write alternative sequels for traditional stories using the same characters and settings, identifying typical phrases and expressions from the story and using these to help them to structure their story-writing.
11	The Spell Which Went Wrong	Fiction: What Next?	• To plot a sequence of episodes modelled on a known story as a plan for writing.
12	George's Ghastly Grandmother	Fiction: My Story	• To write a first-person account, for example: write a character's own account of an incident in a story.
13	Charlotte's Web	Fiction: A Long Story	• To write extended stories based on a plan of incidents, set out in simple chapters with titles and author details. • To use paragraphs to organise the narrative.
14	Cooking in Jórvík	Non-fiction: Information	• To make a simple record of information from texts by completing a chart of information discovered, by listing key words. • To draw together notes from more than one source.
15	Insects	Non-fiction: Reports	• To write simple non-chronological reports from known information (for example, from their own experience or from texts read, using notes they have made to organise and present ideas).
16	Spoon Bells	Non-fiction: Instructions	• To write instructions (for example, rules for games, recipes). • To use a range of organisational devices, for example: lists, dashes, commas for lists in sentences. • To recognise the importance of correct sequence in instructions. • To use writing frames, as appropriate, for support.
17	Too Much Television?	Non-fiction: For or Against	• To make clear notes through making use of simple formats to capture key points, for example: *for* and *against* columns.

Summary of NLS objectives (contd)

Unit	Theme	NLS objectives covered
18 Message Board	Non-fiction: Making Notes	• To make clear notes after discussing the purpose of note-making and looking at simple examples. • To identify key words, phrases or sentences in reading. • To make use of simple formats to capture key points, for example: a flow chart, *for* or *against* columns or matrices in writing or on screen. • To explore ways of writing ideas or messages in shortened forms: for example, lists, headlines, faxes and text messages. • To recognise that some words are more essential to meaning than others. • To identify the intended audience for notes (themselves or others).
19 Two Letters	Non-fiction: Letters	• To write letters, notes and messages linked to work in other subjects. • To write letters to authors about books. • To communicate within the school • To select the appropriate style and vocabulary for the intended reader.
20 Old News	Non-fiction: News Articles	• To experiment with recounting the same event in a variety of ways, for example: in the form of a story, a letter or a news report.
21 Make It Snappy	Non-fiction: Summaries	• To summarise in writing the content of a passage or text and the main point it is making.
22 A Treasure Chest of Words	Poetry: Comparisons	• To investigate and collect suitable words and phrases for writing poems and short descriptions. • To design simple patterns with words, use repetitive phrases and to write imaginative comparisons.
23 Autumn	Poetry: Shape It	• To invent calligrams and a range of shape poems, selecting appropriate words and presenting work carefully. • To contribute to a class collection of calligrams and shape poems.
24 Fast Food	Poetry: New Verses	• To write new or extended verses for performance modelled on performance poetry they have read, for example: using rhythm and repetition.
25 The Witch	Poetry: Sizzling Sounds	• To write poetry which uses alliteration to create effects.
26 Gunerania's Wedding Cake	Poetry: Time for a Laugh	• To write poetry which uses distinctive rhyme patterns to create effects.
27 Girls and Boys	Other Skills: Playscripts	• To write simple playscripts based on their own reading and oral work.
28 Skellig	Other Skills: Create an Effect	• To write openings of stories or chapters linked to, or arising from, reading, which focus on language for creating effects, for example: building up tension or suspense, creating moods or setting scenes.
29 The Worst Witch	Other Skills: A Book Review	• To write book reviews for a specified audience based on evaluations of plot, characters and language.
30 The Toytown Telephone Directory	Other Skills: Alphabetical Order	• To make alphabetically-ordered texts, using information from other subjects, their own experience or information derived from information books.

Book 3 Teacher's Notes

1 Nan's Story

Fiction: Story Ideas

Objective: To generate ideas relevant to a story by brainstorming, word association, and so on.
See also Activity Sheet 3.1

Starting the lesson: Ask the children where they think storytellers get the ideas for their stories. Perhaps they see or hear something which sparks off an idea, and then they begin to think about what might happen. Sometimes other events or talks with other people give them ideas. Tell the children that the passage is about how a grandmother creates stories for her grandchildren; the children's questions shape the ideas for the story and spark off new ideas.

Sentence and word level: Ask the children to identify the questions in the story. How can they tell they are questions? Point out the question marks and compare them with the sentences which answer them (these end with full stops). Encourage the children to read the questions and answers aloud and to notice how the punctuation affects the way in which they read and make sense of the text. Draw attention to the meanings of words. What do the children think of when they hear 'a spell' ('magic'). Point this out in the story and think of other examples of word association.

Plenary session: Invite the children to show their spider diagrams (Activity Sheet 3.1 and section **c**, page 5 of the Pupil's Book) to the class and to talk about how one idea sparked off another. Some of them could read their stories aloud while the others listen and comment on whether the best ideas from the spider diagram were used. Ask them how the diagram and discussion with their group helped them with their writing.

2 Soccer Shadows

Fiction: Story Talk

Objective: Using reading as a model, to write passages of dialogue.

Starting the lesson: Tell the children that this passage is about two boys who have just met for the first time and want to find out about one another. Ask the children how the writer tells the reader about the characters in the story. (Through what they say.) Introduce the words *conversation* and *dialogue*. What information does the dialogue give them about each character, including their names, birth signs, where they are and what they are doing?

Sentence and word level: Ask the children how they can spot the words which are spoken in a text. They should notice the speech marks and, in some places, words to introduce speech, such as *grunt*ed, *came back the reply*, *explained*. Which words are more commonly used to show that someone is going to speak or has spoken? (*said*, *asked*) You could point out that words like this are often missed out, as in this passage. Ask the children to read the dialogue aloud and then to repeat it but with words such as *said*. Point out that this slows down the dialogue.

Plenary session: Invite the children to read out the questions they would ask someone they meet on holiday to find out more about him or her. They could read them with a partner, who could read the answers. Invite them to write up a question (with a question mark at the end). Their partner could write the answer (with a full stop at the end). Look at the passage again and ask the children what they learned about setting out dialogue.

3 No Problem, Davy

Fiction: Story Places

Objective: To develop the use of settings in their own stories by writing short descriptions of known places and writing a description in the style of a familiar story.
See also Activity Sheet 3.2

Starting the lesson: Tell the children that they are going to read a recount which is written in a way which tells the reader about the setting of the story. Read the passage with the children and ask them to compare the punctuation marks with those of the passages in Units 1 and 2. Which punctuation marks does it not use? Why not? Revise the word *recount* and introduce the word *narrative*. Ask the children about the setting of the story and which words tell them this. What picture do they have in their minds?

Sentence and word level: The passage is a recount; things happen and people do things. Ask the children what happens and what the people do, and ask them to identify the words for doing: *branched, buy, drove, like, stood, trying, was moving*. Revise or introduce *verb* for these words. Remind the children that all sentences contain a verb. They could look for the verbs in each sentence. Focus on words which might cause problems (for instance, *bright*) and ask the children to think of other words with the same letter string: *light, night, sight*.

Activity Sheet 3.2 helps them to plan their own recount in the same style as the passage.

Plenary session: Invite the children to read aloud their recounts of travelling through a place in a way which describes it. The others should listen, and identify the words which say what the place is like. Ask them to display their pictures alongside their descriptions. The others could notice how well the description matches the picture and suggest ways in which to improve it.

Book 3 Teacher's Notes

4 Story Openings and Endings

Fiction: Starting and Finishing a Story

Objective: To investigate and collect sentences or phrases for story openings and endings, and to use some of these formal elements in re-telling and story writing.

Starting the lesson: Can the children remember any words with which stories begin? Introduce the term *opening*. Tell them that the opening sentence of a story often uses words such as *Once upon a time* and *One day*, but it might also introduce the setting or a character or say what the story is about.

Can they remember the final words of any stories? They might remember *They all lived happily ever after* from fairy tales. Point out that stories often end with a summary or a sentence suggesting what might happen next or how the events of the story affected the characters.

Sentence and word level: Ask which of the story openings are sentences. Do they make sense? *Once upon a time in London* does not make sense as a sentence, but *There was once a boy named Jack* does. Draw attention to high-frequency words beginning with *o* sounding like *w*: *one*, *once*.

Plenary session: Invite the children to read the opening sentence of their story. Ask the others what it tells them about the setting, the main character and what might happen. Invite the reader to continue (stopping before the final sentence) so the others can check if they were right. What was good about the opening? Can it be improved? Can they suggest a final sentence? Continue so they can compare the final sentence with their suggestions.

5 The Hundred-Mile-An-Hour Dog

Fiction: Paragraphs

Objectives: To begin to organise stories into paragraphs. To begin to use paragraphing in the presentation of dialogue in stories.

See also Activity Sheet 3.3

Starting the lesson: Read the passage and point out that the writer begins the third sentence on a new line. Where, on the line, does it begin? Introduce *indent*. Ask why the writer has split the sentences in this way, and draw attention to what each group of sentences is about. Introduce *paragraph*.

Sentence and word level: Invite a child to talk about his or her pet. Make notes about what he or she says. Group the notes according to what they are about: appearance, food, habits, likes and dislikes. Can the children explain how you have grouped them? Point out that you have grouped the notes to help you to split your writing into paragraphs. Activity Sheet 3.3 helps them to plan their paragraphs about a pet.

Encourage the children to use appropriate strategies for reading the difficult words, for example: reading on, 'leaving a gap' and going back to it after reading the rest of the sentence (as with *accelerate* and *vanished*); splitting words into their separate parts (as with *greyhound* and *whirlwind*).

Plenary session: Re-read the passage and ask which paragraphs they identified as the answers to the questions in section b. Do the others agree?

Invite the children to explain how they split their own stories into paragraphs. The stories could be displayed in a class book; encourage the children to read them and to notice the paragraphing. You could leave a notebook beside the class storybook, in which the children could write comments.

6 The Story of Persephone

Fiction: What Happened?

Objectives: To plan the main points as a structure for story-writing. To consider how to capture points in a few words which can be elaborated later. To discuss different methods of planning.

See also Activity Sheet 3.4

Starting the lesson: Tell the children they are going to read a myth. Do they know what a myth is? It is an ancient story of gods and goddesses about a problem connected with humans and it often gives an explanation of something familiar. Read the passage and ask them what happens in it. List the responses. Introduce and explain the term *main events* and ask them if they have listed the most important events. Help them to distinguish between background information and events. Talk about the themes of the story and explain them.

Activity Sheet 3.4 helps them to write the main points of another Greek myth (section c).

Sentence and word level: The passage contains some long sentences. Copy some of them with the commas deleted and ask a child to read them aloud. The others should listen and notice where they stumble or have difficulty. Ask the children to find the commas in the original version and to say how they help. Encourage them to use commas in their own writing.

Look at the plurals in the passage and write their singular forms. Ask the children how the words were changed.

Plenary session: Invite a child whose work is a good example to read the original and then to read his or her own version. The others could comment on how well the main events are covered. Are any missing? Are they in the right order? Comment on how the storyteller's notes helped.

Book 3 Teacher's Notes

7 Goldilocks

Fiction: Putting It In Order

Objective: To describe and sequence key incidents in a variety of ways, for example: by listing, charting, mapping, making simple storyboards.

Starting the lesson: Ask the children if they know the story of *Goldilocks and the Three Bears*. Introduce or revise *fairy tale* and *traditional tale*. Invite the children to re-tell the story, drawing out the main events. Look at the story map; point to places on the map and ask them what happened in each place. Discuss how the story map helps them to tell the events in the correct order and to include some description of the setting.

Sentence and word level: The children could draw the bears, their tableware and furniture in order of size and say which are bigger, biggest, larger, largest, smaller, smallest, taller, tallest, and so on. Point out the formation of comparatives and superlatives and how the endings sometimes change before *-er* or *-est* is added.

Plenary session: Ask the children how their story maps of *Puss in Boots* helped them to re-tell the story. Did the map help them to put their notes into the correct order? Did it remind them about the places in which the events of the story happened? Would it help in re-telling a story in which everything happened in the same place (for example, *Cinderella*)?

8 The Legend of Rama and Sita

Fiction: Story People

Objective: To write portraits of characters, using a story text to describe behaviour and characteristics, and to present portraits in a variety of ways, for example: as posters, labelled diagrams or letters to friends about the characters.

Starting the lesson: Ask the children if they know what a legend is. Tell them that it is a traditional story about heroes from the past, possibly based on real people and events. It might have been changed over the years. Like myths, legends often have themes such as power and weakness, good and evil, wisdom and foolishness. This one is about good and evil.

Sentence and word level: Revise adjectives and ask them to think of some adjectives to describe the characters in the story. They should support their answers with examples from the passage. Introduce interesting adjectives: *fearsome*, *gentle*, *loyal*, *terrifying*, *vile*.

The children could compile a word bank of new words from the passage, for example: *demon*, *fawn*, *heir*. Encourage them to use the Look, Say, Cover, Write, Check spelling strategy to learn their spellings.

Plenary session: Ask the children what they have learned about legends and their characters. Invite them to read their letter from a monkey. Does it describe Ravana's character or just re-tell the story? Revise the difference between re-telling a story and describing a character. If necessary, provide additional activities to help children who have difficulty with this, for example: they could design a 'Wanted' poster about Ravana.

9 The Parable of the Seeds

Fiction: Story Plan

Objective: To write a story plan for their own myth, fable or traditional tale, using a story theme from reading but substituting different characters or changing the setting.

See also Activity Sheet 3.5

Starting the lesson: Tell the children that the passage comes from the Christian Bible (it is a parable which Jesus told) and that a parable is a story used to explain something. Read the passage and discuss its meaning. Ask them to name the four places where the seeds fell. Which three outcomes are bad and which is good? What did each of these mean about people who heard the words of God? Point out why Jesus chose the sowing of seeds as the subject of the parable: he was talking to people from farming communities. Talk about a different audience for a modern parable: for instance, cooks. Invite them to suggest ideas for a parable, with the same meaning, about a cake being baked: it might turn out soggy, it might burn, flies might land on it or it might turn out to be delicious. Which outcomes are bad and which is good? Help them to relate these to people who hear the words of God, as in the original.

Activity Sheet 3.5 helps them to plan a modern version of a parable (section **c**).

Sentence and word level: Help the children to work out the meanings of new words from their context, for instance: *produced*. Focus on the adjectives used to describe the seeds and the shoots which grew from them (*weak*, *healthy*, *rich*, *strong*), and ask the children to think of other adjectives to describe them. Discuss the adjectives they could use in another version of the parable.

Point out the high-frequency words which need to be learned: *going*, *out*, *they*, *were*, *where*. Others can be learned by their initial phoneme and their shape: *edge*, *fell*, *shone*, *strong*. In other words, the children could look for 'words within words': *farmer*, *soil*, *sprang*.

Plenary session: Invite the children to read aloud their parable. The others should listen and explain it. Ask them to identify the audience and to say how the parable is suited to the things which are familiar to them. Revise how parables are different from other stories. The children should be able to say what a parable is for.

Book 3 Teacher's Notes

10 The Little Match Girl

Fiction: What If …?

Objective: To write alternative sequels for traditional stories using the same characters and settings, identifying typical phrases and expressions from the story and using these to help them to structure their story-writing.

See also Activity Sheet 3.6

Starting the lesson: Revise story settings: the place and the time, the weather and anything which affects the place. Tell the children that this story was written in Denmark about 150 years ago. Ask them how they feel about the little match girl. What could have happened to make the story happier? List their responses. New characters could have appeared in the story. What could they have done? The setting could have been altered. Activity Sheet 3.6 will help.

Sentence and word level: Revise capital letters and ask them to identify words in the passage which have capital letters and to say why. Why should *Grandma* have a capital letter in *Grandma, take me with you* but not *grandmother* in *her grandmother*?

Point out words with common suffixes such as *-ing*, *-ly*, *-ness* and *-y* (*snowing, bitterly, darkness, rosy*) and ask the children to identify the root words and how these words are changed.

Plenary session: Invite the children to read aloud their new version of the story with its happy ending. Ask the others to identify the changes (the setting, characters and events). Do they prefer the happy or the sad ending? Discuss ways of keeping the story sad almost to the end and then giving it a surprisingly happy ending. What could happen at the very last minute?

11 The Spell Which Went Wrong

Fiction: What Next?

Objective: To plot a sequence of episodes modelled on a known story as a plan for writing.

See also Activity Sheet 3.7

Starting the lesson: Tell the children that the passage is from an adventure story. Do they know any Mr Majeika stories? What do they know? He is a teacher who casts magic spells — which usually go wrong. The problems they cause usually have a happy ending. Ask the children if the passage is from the beginning of the story. How can they tell? (Mr Majeika talks about 'the spell'; this suggests that something has happened before this event.) Read the rest of the passage. Do the children think it is from the end of the story? (The problem in the story has still to be resolved, so the passage cannot be from the end.) Activity Sheet 3.7 helps them to write the next part of the story.

Sentence and word level: Point to an apostrophe and ask the children if they know what it is called. Introduce *apostrophe* and ask them to find some in the passage. Explain that an apostrophe can be used in a word which has been shortened, to show where letters have been missed out: *can't, didn't, don't, I'm, that's, there's*.

Point out words in the passage with silent letters: *light, whole*. Can they think of other words with silent letters?

Plenary session: Talk about how the problem in the passage can be solved and about the new problem which they introduced. Does their sequel have the right kind of things happening? (Mr Majeika could cause problems by getting his spells wrong.) They could give their stories to a partner who could write the solution. Continue at other times or for homework. The stories could be displayed or made into a class story book.

12 George's Ghastly Grandmother

Fiction: My Story

Objective: To write a first-person account, for example: write a character's own account of an incident in a story.

Starting the lesson: Display some books by Roald Dahl; include leaflets and posters from the publishers. Give the children time to look at them and to talk about them. What do they know about Roald Dahl? They could look for information in the books. Tell them that the passage is from an adventure story. Read the passage and ask them how George feels about his grandmother. How can they tell? Look for descriptions as well as statements such as *he hated Grandma* and *he was frightened: he was shaking* (with hatred), *he wanted to explode her away*.

Sentence and word level: Ask them to look for the words in the passage which are used instead of the nouns *George* and *Grandma* (*he, him, himself, she, her*). Which pronouns does George use for himself? (*I, me*) Discuss how to change the passage as if George were telling the story. (The pronouns *I, me, my* and *myself* would be used.)

Look for synonyms in the passage, especially where repetition is used for effect: *terrific, tremendous, whopping; explosion, shocker*.

Plenary session: Invite the children to talk about the changes they made. Introduce and explain *third person* and *first person*. You could also explain what *second person* means and why stories are not usually written in the second person. They could read from their stories; the others should notice if the story keeps to the first person all the way through.

Book 3 Teacher's Notes

13 Charlotte's Web
Fiction: A Long Story

Objectives: To write extended stories based on a plan of incidents, set out in simple chapters with titles and author details. To use paragraphs to organise the narrative.

See also Activity Sheet 3.8

Starting the lesson: Display some books which are split into chapters, including *Charlotte's Web* by E.B. White. The children could look at the titles of the chapters or skim them to find out what they are about. Discuss a book you are reading with the class; ask what some of the chapters are about. Write up their responses in the form of summaries of the chapters. Tell them they are going to read summaries of four chapters from *Charlotte's Web*. Show a copy of the book and read the blurb so they know what it is about. If any of them have read it, they could tell the others about it.

Sentence and word level: Ask the children to compile from their reading a word bank of useful words for linking events in a story: *after that, first, meanwhile, next, then*. Encourage them to use these words in their own stories.

Point out the specialist vocabulary about farming used in the passage: *barn, orchard, piglet*. They could look up any new words. Point out that they do not need to start from *A* in a dictionary if they are looking for a word beginning with *O*. Encourage them to open it in roughly the right place. Ask them to research the topic on which their own story is based and to list any new words.

Plenary session: Discuss how the story plan (Activity Sheet 3.8) will help the children to write a long story. Ask them to read the titles and summaries of the chapters they have planned and to identify the main events.

14 Cooking in Jórvík
Non-fiction: Information

Objectives: To make a simple record of information from texts by completing a chart of information discovered, by listing key words. To draw together notes from more than one source.

Starting the lesson: Ask the children to sort some books into *Fiction* and *Non-fiction*. How can they tell the difference? (Fiction books tell stories sometimes based on real places and even real people but usually the events are made up. The style of the books: the illustrations and captions, the index, and the way in which they are written are different.) Select a fiction and a non-fiction book on a similar theme (for example, *The 101 Dalmatians* and an information book about dogs). Point out that non-fiction books give facts which can be checked. Read the passage and ask what shows that it is an information book. What facts does it give? How can they be checked?

Sentence and word level: Revise sentences (they start with a capital letter, end with a full stop and contain a verb). Point out that in notes they need not use capital letters (except for names) or full stops; they need only write the important verbs and can miss out unimportant words. Help them to write the first sentence of the passage in notes: *Norse settled Jórvík 10th century*. Show them how to use symbols such as arrows to replace words: *rich → iron spit for roasting meat*.

Encourage the children to collect new words from their reading: they could list them in a subject word bank.

Plenary session: Discuss how the children recorded information from different sources for their report. Help them to sort the information, perhaps by using arrows to link points. Then invite them to write sentences. Point out that they have written their own sentences rather than just copying.

15 Insects
Non-fiction: Reports

Objective: To write simple non-chronological reports from known information (for example, from their own experience or from texts read, using notes they have made to organise and present ideas).

Starting the lesson: Revise *fiction, non-fiction* and *fact*. Tell them that they are going to read a passage from a non-fiction text called a non-chronological report (a text which gives information about something). Ask them to look at the title and to say what it gives information about. How can they tell it is an information text? They should notice the labelled diagrams with captions. Point out that it is from a book with chapters about different insects and that each chapter has a title to help readers find information. Ask them what each paragraph in the passage is about and to find some facts about insects from it.

Sentence and word level: Revise *caption* and *label*. Identify examples of each of these in the passage and say how they help the reader.

Ask them to identify new words in the passage and to say what they mean (most are explained). Where else in the book could new words be explained? Revise glossaries. Which words from the passage would they put into a glossary? They could collect new words from their reading and list them in a subject word bank about insects.

Plenary session: Ask the children to read out facts from their charts. Where could they check them? (From other information books, CD-ROMs and videos about insects and by studying the insects themselves.) How did the passage help them to decide which animals are insects?

16 Spoon Bells

Non-fiction: Instructions

Objectives: To write instructions (for example, rules for games, recipes). To use a range of organisational devices, for example: lists, dashes, commas for lists in sentences. To recognise the importance of correct sequence in instructions. To use writing frames, as appropriate, for support.

See also Activity Sheet 3.9

Starting the lesson: Provide texts of different kinds: fiction, reports, recipes, timetables, instructions and travel directions. Ask the children to find those which tell people how to do something. Look at the covers, headings, illustrations and indexes, and say what they tell people how to do. Introduce *instructions*. What instructions have the children used? Ask them to look at the title, illustrations and captions in the passage and to say what the instructions are for. Ask them to try following the instructions. What will they need? What will they do first? Ask them how good the instructions were. How did they know in which order to carry out the steps? How did they know what to do?

Sentence and word level: Ask how the verbs in instructions are different from verbs in other texts. You need not introduce *imperative* at this stage, but the children should realise that the verbs *tell* the reader what to do; in the other texts they *record* what people or things did or do.

Point out the spelling of *metre*. Can they think of a homophone for it and give its meaning? (*Meter*, as in a gas meter.) Can they spell these words which end with the same sound: *heater, letter, litre, poster, sister, water*? Point out that *-ter* is more common than *-tre*, and encourage them to use the Look, Say, Cover, Write, Check spelling strategy to learn the spellings of words ending in *-tre*.

Plenary session: Ask the children to give their instructions (Activity Sheet 3.9) to others to read. Ask the reader if he or she can tell what the instructions are for and what materials are needed. How? Can they see easily in what order to follow them? (Numbers, arrows and boxes help.)

17 Too Much Television?

Non-fiction: For or Against

Objective: To make clear notes through making use of simple formats to capture key points, for example: *for* and *against* columns.

See also Activity Sheet 3.10

Starting the lesson: Revise the meaning of *fact*. Introduce the word *opinion* and explain that it means what people think about something. The children could take turns to read aloud the words in the speech bubbles. Ask them to identify the people who think children should not watch too much television, and how they can tell. Who thinks it's good for children to watch television, and how can they tell? Introduce the word *argument*.

Sentence and word level: Ask the children to find quick ways of writing notes for their survey. They could try deleting words from sentences to see if they are essential to the meaning.

Draw attention to high-frequency words with difficult spellings such as *could, should* and *would*.

Plenary session: Invite the children to comment on how helpful they found a chart for collecting opinions (Activity Sheet 3.10). Did it help them to group and summarise them?

18 Message Board

Non-fiction: Making Notes

Objectives: To make clear notes after discussing the purpose of note-making and looking at simple examples. To identify key words, phrases or sentences in reading. To make use of simple formats to capture key points, for example: a flow chart, *for* or *against* columns, or matrices in writing or on screen. To explore ways of writing ideas or messages in shortened forms, for example: lists, headlines, faxes and text messages. To recognise that some words are more essential to meaning than others. To identify the intended audience for notes (themselves or others).

Starting the lesson: Ask the children to sort a collection of notes: memos, personal reminders, shopping lists, notes to delivery people, and so on: 'for someone else' and 'for the writer only'. Discuss when people write notes to others, and why. When might they write a note to themselves?

Sentence and word level: Introduce or revise addressing and signing off letters and notes (explain *address, greeting* and *sign off*). Discuss when each style is appropriate. Compare the two forms of lists which the children will come across: those written across the page with the items separated by commas and those with one item written below another without commas.

The children could compile a word bank of greetings and signing-off expressions and collect other useful expressions to use in notes and letters.

Plenary session: Ask the children about the audience and purpose of the notes they wrote. (They are for the writer only to read, to help him or her to remember a list of things.) Encourage them to write notes at school to remember what to bring in to school or to do.

Book 3 Teacher's Notes

19 Two Letters

Non-fiction: Letters

Objectives: To write letters, notes and messages linked to work in other subjects. To write letters to authors about books. To communicate within the school. To select the appropriate style and vocabulary for the intended reader.

See also Activity Sheet 3.11

Starting the lesson: Provide some formal and informal letters giving and requesting information, complaining, congratulating, thanking, and so on. Ask the children to sort them by purpose. Revise ways of addressing letters. Can they tell from how the letters are addressed and signed off whether the reader knows the writer or is a close friend or family member? Tell them they are going to read two letters about similar topics, written for different purposes, for different readers and in different styles.

Sentence and word level: Point out the pronouns in the postcard and the letter and how they agree with the verbs. Point out that when people write a letter they use the pronouns *I* and *me* for themselves. Introduce *first person*, *second person* and *third person* and ask the children to copy extracts from the postcard and the letter, changing the person. They should change the verb as well as the pronoun.

Collect words for letters: for asking, complaining, congratulating and thanking.

Plenary session: Ask the children about the changes they made to the postcard to convert it into a more formal letter (Activity Sheet 3.11). They should have written complete sentences and replaced contracted words with their full versions and the greeting and signing off should be more formal — the recipient should be addressed by title and family name rather than personal name, and the letter should be signed off *yours sincerely* and the sender's full name.

20 Old News

Non-fiction: News Articles

Objective: To experiment with recounting the same event in a variety of ways, for example: in the form of a story, a letter or a news report.

See also Activity Sheet 3.12

Starting the lesson: Revise *recounts* and their purpose (to tell the reader about something which has happened). Revise the terms *fiction*, *non-fiction* and *fact* and ask the children which of these apply to newspaper articles. Read the passage and draw attention to how the facts are reported (there is narrative and a quotation). Note that the introduction gives background information about Caratacus and what was going on in Britain. Discuss the ending; it gives the reader the latest news and suggests that there might be more to come.

Sentence and word level: Look for the words which tell about the order in which things happened: *for two days*, *in the end*, *now*, *this time*, *until*. Collect others to use in their own writing. Discuss how the reports present the facts and ask them to find the quotation in the passage. How can they tell it is a quotation? Revise the punctuation and layout of speech. They could show the spoken words by drawing a cartoon-style picture of the speaker with a speech bubble.

Ask them to use a dictionary to look up new words, and a thesaurus to find synonyms. Make a class glossary on 'Invaders', linked with work in history.

Plenary session: Ask the children about the changes they made to turn a written account of an event in history into a newspaper-style report (Activity Sheet 3.12). How did they change the layout? Introduce the word *columns* (as used in print). How did they introduce the topic? Did they give the background information? How did they end it? Did they give the latest news and suggest that there might be more to come?

21 Make It Snappy

Non-fiction: Summaries

Objective: To summarise in writing the content of a passage or text and the main point it is making.

Starting the lesson: Read headlines and ask the children to predict what the report will be about. Cut the headlines off some reports and ask them to match them to the reports. Read the passages and ask what each report is about. How are these different from the passage in Unit 20? (They are about the present day and are non-chronological reports, not recounts.) Revise *non-chronological report*, *recount*, *fiction*, *non-fiction* and *fact*. Which terms apply to the passage?

Sentence and word level: Compare the ways in which headlines and the text are written and point out words which are sometimes missed out to make headlines brief: *a*, *an*, *the*. The children could write headlines for other work.

Provide thesauruses so that the children can find synonyms for words such as *normally*, *opportunity*.

Plenary session: Ask the children to read the headline for their report. Can the others predict what it will be about? Ask them to read out the subheadings. The others could say what they think will be in each section. Discuss how well the headline and subheadings summed up the report.

14

22 A Treasure Chest of Words

Poetry: Comparisons

Objectives: To investigate and collect suitable words and phrases for writing poems and short descriptions. To design simple patterns with words, use repetitive phrases and to write imaginative comparisons.

Starting the lesson: Read the comparisons with the children and point out the words which show that they are comparisons: *a ... of a ...*, *as ... as ...*, *like*, *than*. Ask them what is being compared with what. What impression does that create? For instance, *tall as a telegraph pole* indicates tall, slim and straight (rather than massive, bulky or towering). Show the children other pictures for which they can suggest comparisons: a hat piled with artificial fruit, a brightly striped tie, a bird such as a stork which has very long legs, a derelict house, a fast car.

Sentence and word level: Revise sentences; they have to contain a verb, begin with a capital letter and end with a full stop and make sense. Compare the lines of poetry with sentences. Point out that poetry does not have to be written in complete sentences.

Set up a database of comparisons to which the children can add as they come across them. Classify the comparisons according to the 'comparison words' (*a ... of a ...*, *as ... as ...*, *like*, *than*).

Plenary session: Invite the children to share the pictures they drew for the comparisons in section **a**. They could display them and ask the others to identify the comparison. How well does the picture express the comparison? Also invite the children to share the comparisons they wrote in a poem about an old house, a child in a bad temper or a spider (section **c**).

23 Autumn

Poetry: Shape It

Objectives: To invent calligrams and a range of shape poems, selecting appropriate words and presenting work carefully. To contribute to a class collection of calligrams and shape poems.

See also Activity Sheet 3.13

Starting the lesson: Read the shape poem with the children and ask them how it is different from other poems. Is the shape important? What effect does it create? Discuss how the shape reflects the effect created by the words of the poem. Ask the children to close the textbook. Give them a large leaf shape and ask them to write on it a word about autumn. Help them to arrange the words as a poem, which could be displayed. Introduce the word *calligram*.

Sentence and word level: Revise adjectives. While making notes for fire poems, the children could use a thesaurus to look up synonyms for adjectives about fire, flames, burning, and so on: *crimson*, *forked*, *glowing*, *orange*, *scarlet*, *searing*. Revise verbs; consider different verbs with similar meanings and ask the children to use a thesaurus to find others: *crackle*, *flicker*, *gleam*, *glow*, *lick*, *spark*.

Plenary session: Invite the children to share their poems about a fire. They could first read it aloud and then display it. Discuss the effect of the poem. Awe-inspiring? Comforting? Fascinating? Frightening or menacing? Does the shape add to the effect of the poem, and how? How can the shape of the flames be altered to make them look menacing or comforting?

24 Fast Food

Poetry: New Verses

Objective: To write new or extended verses for performance modelled on performance poetry they have read, for example: using rhythm and repetition.

See also Activity Sheet 3.14

Starting the lesson: Read the fast food poem with the children. Different children could read different verses, with the whole group joining in the chorus. Introduce the term *chorus* and ask the children if they know what it means. Discuss how they can recognise a chorus in a poem or song. Ask them to identify the rhyming words. Ask them to suggest rhymes for *spicy dips* (fish and chips), *T-bone steaks* (fruit cakes, fairy cakes), *home-made* (lemonade), *boiled ham* (strawberry jam). Encourage the children to try out ideas for rhymes with a partner.

Sentence and word level: Investigate different ways of spelling the same phoneme (*a-e*, *ai*; *ay*, *oa*, *o-e*, *ow*; *ea*, *e-e*, *ee*, *ie*) and collect examples of words containing them.

Explore homophones: *bean/been*, *coarse/course*, *hoarse/horse*, *scene/seen*, *their/there*, *wear/where*. Encourage the children to collect others.

Plenary session: Invite the children to share their new verses for the fast food poem (Activity Sheet 3.14). They could read them aloud with a partner, with the whole group joining in the chorus.

Ask the others to notice if the rhymes are in the right places. They could comment on whether the rhythm is correct and, if not, how the poem could be changed. The class could combine their verses to create a long fast food poem.

Book 3 Teacher's Notes

25 The Witch

Poetry: Sizzling Sounds

Objective: To write poetry which uses alliteration to create effects.

Starting the lesson: Read 'The Witch' to the children. Did they enjoy it? What did they like or dislike about it? Ask them if they liked the sounds of the words. Ask them to listen to the beginnings of the words. What do they notice? Point out the words in the first line which begin with the same consonant sound (*fearsome flight*) and discuss the effect of this repetition of sound. Ask them to look for other words which begin with the same consonant sounds. Introduce the term *alliteration* for the repetition of initial consonants: *wild/wicked/witch, cackling/crone, ten/twisted/toes, sweeps/sky*.

Sentence and word level: Investigate the punctuation and layout of poems and compare them with narrative or descriptive text. Ask the children to identify the differences. Discuss the effects of these differences and relate them to the purpose of the text.

Encourage them to record new words they come across in their reading in a personal word log (alphabetically under headings such as *Nouns, Adjectives, Verbs, Expressions of feelings*, and so on).

Show them how to create a table in Word and to use it for putting each set into alphabetical order.

Plenary session: Invite the children to share their ghost poems. The others should listen for alliterative words, such as *slithering/slipping/slinking, dashing/darting/daring, whispering/whistling/wailing, clomping/clanging/clattering*. Ask them to use what they learned about shape poems (Unit 23) to create a shape which adds to the effect of their poem.

26 Gunerania's Wedding Cake

Poetry: Time for a Laugh

Objective: To write poetry which uses distinctive rhyme patterns to create effects.

See also Activity Sheet 3.15

Starting the lesson: Tell the children they are going to read part of a poem by primary school children. With their teacher, they created a rhyme pattern for their poem which helped to make it lively and funny. Read the verses to them. What did they like best? Ask them what they found funny. They could identify the lines which are repeated with slight changes. What changes are made to the repeated lines? Ask them to look for a pattern.

Activity Sheet 3.15 helps them to write new verses for the poem.

Sentence and word level: Revise the use of commas in making meaning clear. The children could try re-writing a verse of the poem without its commas and trying to read it. What difference do the commas make? Ask them to re-read some of their own work to see if commas would help to make its meaning clear.

Encourage them to make rhyme banks from which they can select words to use in their poems. Discuss the best ways of arranging them.

Plenary session: Invite the children to share their verses for 'Gunerania's Wedding Cake'. Check that they have rhymes in all the right places: at the ends of the appropriate lines and within some lines. Let them have fun reading their verses aloud at other times, with a partner, and making up lines which make them laugh. They could display their verses. You could return to the poem during another lesson.

27 Girls and Boys

Other Skills: Playscripts

Objective: To write simple playscripts based on their own reading and oral work.

Starting the lesson: Tell the children that they are going to read part of a playscript based on the story *Bill's New Frock* by Anne Fine. Any children who have read it could say what they remember: the main character, other characters, setting and plot. Introduce the words *cast, lines, props* (short for *properties*), *scene* and *stage directions*. Read the opening section of the passage and invite four children to take the parts. How do they know what to do, what to say and how to say it? Point out the stage directions. Ask the children how a producer would know what setting and props to make for the play.

Sentence and word level: Ask the children to compare how dialogue is written in the novel (see page 57 of the Pupil's Book) and the playscript based on it. They should notice that the novel uses speech marks and indents the line when a new speaker begins. It uses words to show when someone is about to speak or has just spoken. *Said* does not appear in the extract on page 57, but the children can find another word which is used instead. They should notice how each new speaker is introduced in the playscript and how a change of font helps to distinguish between the speaker's name, the spoken words and the stage directions.

Ask them to collect useful expressions of surprise, anger, exasperation, and so on, which can be used in playscripts.

Plenary session: Ask the children to swap playscripts. How well can someone else choose the characters, and props? How well can the cast read their lines?

Book 3 Teacher's Notes

28 Skellig
Other Skills: Create an Effect

Objective: To write openings of stories or chapters linked to, or arising from, reading, which focus on language for creating effects, for example: building up tension or suspense, creating moods or setting scenes.

See also Activity Sheet 3.16

Starting the lesson: Read the passage and ask the children about its atmosphere. Is it exciting, funny, happy, mysterious or sad? Or would they use a different word to describe it? Draw out how the writer creates a sense of mystery. The stillness of the night is created by expressions such as *the moon hung over the city*. The sense of mystery is created by the descriptions of the colours in the scene. Other words which add to the sense of stillness and mystery are *whispered* and *saw nothing*.

Sentence and word level: List the adjectives used in the passage. The children could look for contrasting adjectives.

Ask them to collect verbs which they can use instead of commonly-used verbs such as *looked*, *said* or *went*. Discuss the effects created by different verbs.

Plenary session: Ask the children to read from their altered versions of the passage (Activity Sheet 3.16). Which words did they change? Suggest how the punctuation could be changed to create an exciting effect, for example: in the last line, exclamation marks could replace the comma and full stop at the ends of the two sets of spoken words.

29 The Worst Witch
Other Skills: A Book Review

Objective: To write book reviews for a specified audience based on evaluations of plot, characters and language.

Starting the lesson: Revise 'book' vocabulary: *author, characters, cover, ending, illustrator, main events, opening, publisher, review, title page*. If they have read *The Worst Witch*, what do they remember about it? Read the heading and the first paragraph and ask them how these help readers who do not know the book. Ask them what each paragraph is about: the opening and the setting and what the book is about; the main character and the other characters; the main events and an idea about the ending. Does the review say exactly how the story ends? Discuss how this would spoil it for anyone who has not read it.

Sentence and word level: Revise the words which join sentences: *and, because, but, however, meanwhile, so, that, then, which, who*.

Point out difficult letter combinations, such as *ch* pronounced *k* in *character*. They could look for other examples with the same letter combinations: *echo, Christmas, Christine*. They could also split compound words into their two separate words: *anything, headteacher*.

Plenary session: List questions to which the children's book reviews should provide the answers. Ask them to use the questions to check their reviews: Who is the author? Who is the illustrator? What is the setting? What kind of story is it and what is it about? Who is the main character and what is he or she like? Who are the other characters and what are they like? What kinds of things happen in the story and what is the main event? What kind of ending does it have?

30 The Toytown Telephone Directory
Other Skills: Alphabetical Order

Objective: To make alphabetically-ordered texts, using information from other subjects, their own experience or information derived from information books.

Starting the lesson: Show the children a telephone directory and ask them where they would open it to find someone whose name begins with W. Near the back, near the front or near the middle? Why? Discuss the order of the names in the telephone directory. Read the passage and point out the names which begin with the same letter. How do we know which should come first?

TIP: Create a table in Word by using TABLE→INSERT→TABLE and selecting two columns. Add rows by hitting the TAB key at the end of a row. Key family names into the first and personal names in the second column. To arrange them in alphabetical order, select TABLE→SORT→COLUMN 2 and ASCENDING.

Sentence and word level: Practise alphabetical order by first letter and show the children what to do about names which begin with the same letter (the second letter is taken into account). Ask them where, on this page, they would add Georgie Porgy and why.

Encourage them to try to spell people's names by thinking about how the same phonemes are spelled in other words and then deciding if they look right. Help them to recognise names by shape and other characteristics.

Plenary session: Ask the children how they put a list of their groups' names into alphabetical order using a word-processed table. How would they do this without using SORT on the table? Discuss how they can ensure that all the names are in the correct order. Select the name of another child and ask them where to add this name without using the computer.

Activity Sheet 3.1

Name: _____

Story Ideas

Use this sheet to write ideas for a story about a strange problem for someone at school.

Details about the problem

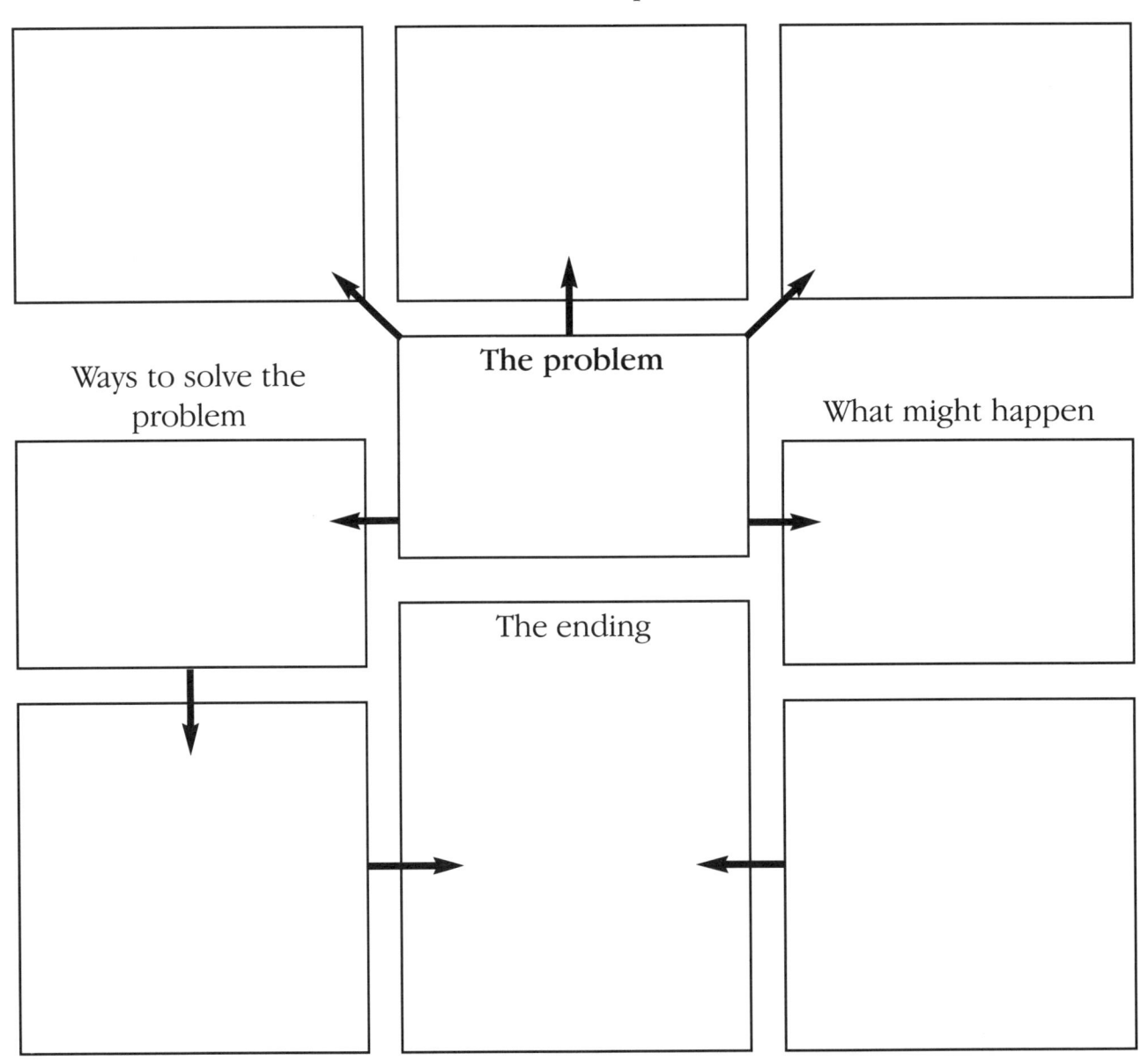

Ways to solve the problem

The problem

What might happen

The ending

Teacher's notes
Supports Unit 1 of Pupil's Book 3. Discuss what might have happened to the character in the story. Ask the children to write a summary of the problem in the central box. They can then add details: what might happen to the character, what will his or her family do, will people worry about them, what dangers face them, how might they feel? Encourage the children to think of exciting solutions and what might happen as a result. Then ask them to decide how they want the episode to end.

Key to Writing Teacher's Book 2. Text © Christine Moorcroft and Les Ray 2003.
Illustrations © Letts Educational 2003. Published by Letts Educational 2003

Activity Sheet 3.2

Name: _____

A Story Setting

Think about a place you have visited. Write some notes about it.

Where does the story take place?	
When?	What is the weather like?

Word bank		
Nouns for the things in the place	Adjectives to describe the place and the things in it	Verbs for moving through the place

The first sentence of your description:

Teacher's notes
Supports Unit 3 of Pupil's Book 3. Ask the children to picture the scene. They could talk to a partner about it. Encourage them to ask their partner questions about the scene; they could ask for details about the place, the objects and people in it, the weather, the time of day, the time of the year and so on. Encourage them to think about the setting as if they are moving through it; they should list verbs as well as nouns and adjectives.

Activity Sheet 3.3

Name: _____

My Pet

Use this sheet to plan your paragraphs for a story about a pet.

Paragraph 1 Introduce the pet.

What kind of animal is it?

Paragraph 2 What is the pet like?

What does it do? What does it like?

Paragraph 3 What problems does the pet cause?

Paragraph 4 What do other people think of the pet?

Paragraph 5 How do your parents try to persuade you to look after the pet?

Teacher's notes
Supports Unit 5 of Pupil's Book 3. After the children have introduced the pet, ask them to say what is special about it: what makes it different from an ordinary dog, cat, etc., and the problems which arise from its special nature (for example, it could be very big, very small, very clever or able to talk). Each paragraph should be about a different aspect of the pet.

Activity Sheet 3.4

Name: _____

The Main Points

Use this sheet to help you to re-tell a story. Write notes.

Main points
Headings:

Details

Write a heading for each point. Then add details.

Teacher's notes
Supports Unit 6 of Pupil's Book 3. You could ask the class to work on the same story — a myth or legend they have read during shared reading sessions. Ask them what they think are the main points. Write up their responses as brief headings and then ask the class if they agree. What do they think should be changed? Ask them what needs to be added to help someone who has not read the story to understand what it is about.

Activity Sheet 3.5

Name: _____

Parable Plan

Use this sheet to plan a modern version of a parable.

Setting *Where?*	Audience *Who will listen?*

What will stand for the words of God?

Main events: *What happens?*

1	2
3	4

Explanation *What does the parable mean?*

Teacher's notes
Supports Unit 9 of Pupil's Book 3. Ask the children to suggest a modern setting for the parable. What might the audience have in common, for example: their work or a hobby? They might be footballers, singers, police officers, bakers or any other group the children find interesting. Ask them what might be meaningful for these people instead of seeds, for example: goal kicks or penalties, songs, crimes or cakes. Discuss what might happen to these things and how this can be linked to the parable.

Activity Sheet 3.6

Name: _____

What If ...?

Think of a new character who could change the ending of The Little Match Girl.

The new character

Name: _____

Description: _____
_____
_____
_____

Picture

Where he or she comes from: _____

What the new character does: _____
_____
_____
_____
_____

How this changes the ending: _____
_____
_____
_____
_____
_____
_____

Teacher's notes
Supports Unit 10 of Pupil's Book 3. Ask the children if they had hoped anything would happen to help the little match girl while they were reading the story. Who could have helped? How? For example, someone could have opened the door of the house and found her earlier. He or she could have invited her into the house, and so on.

Key to Writing Teacher's Book 2. Text © Christine Moorcroft and Les Ray 2003.
Illustrations © Letts Educational 2003. Published by Letts Educational 2003

Activity Sheet 3.7

Name: _____

What Next?

Use this sheet to plan another event in the story of Mr Majeika.

The story so far:

What has happened?	Where?

Who are the characters?

What is their problem?

What next?

How can they solve the problem?

What other problem might they face?

Teacher's notes
Supports Unit 11 of Pupil's Book 3. Discuss the problem which has happened in the story so far. To whom has it happened? How can they solve the problem? Discuss other problems which could arise from Mr Majeika's spells going wrong.

Key to Writing Teacher's Book 2. Text © Christine Moorcroft and Les Ray 2003.
Illustrations © Letts Educational 2003. Published by Letts Educational 2003

Activity Sheet 3.8

Name: _____

A Long Story

Use this sheet to plan a long story.

Chapter 1 Title: _____
Notes:

Chapter 2 Title: _____
Notes:

Chapter 3 Title: _____
Notes:

Chapter 4 Title: _____
Notes:

Teacher's notes
Supports Unit 13 of Pupil's Book 3. Point out that it is easier to write a long story if a writer has a plan to follow. A plan helps him or her to remember what is going to happen in the story and to split it into chapters. Encourage the children to tell one another their stories and to write notes as they do so. This sheet helps them to think of titles and write notes for four chapters.

Key to Writing Teacher's Book 2. Text © Christine Moorcroft and Les Ray 2003.
Illustrations © Letts Educational 2003. Published by Letts Educational 2003

Activity Sheet 3.9

Name: _____

Do This!

Use this sheet to help you to write instructions for making something.

How to make _____

You need:

Picture

Do this:

1	4
2	5
3	You will now have _____ _____ _____ .

Teacher's notes
Supports Unit 16 of Pupil's Book 3. Point out that instructions for making something should begin by saying clearly what they are for and include a picture of what it should look like. So that the reader can have everything he or she needs, there should be a list of all the equipment and materials needed. To help the reader to follow them, the instructions should be written in the correct order. At the end, there should be a statement describing the finished product.

Key to Writing Teacher's Book 2. Text © Christine Moorcroft and Les Ray 2003.
Illustrations © Letts Educational 2003. Published by Letts Educational 2003

Activity Sheet 3.10

Name: _____

For or Against

Use this sheet to collect opinions.

The question: _____

Opinions	
For	Against

Summary of the argument:

Teacher's notes
Supports Unit 17 of Pupil's Book 3. Decide with the children what question is to be considered. They could collect opinions by talking to others in the class and making notes on the appropriate side of the chart. Each 'for' or 'against' entry should be supported by a reason or evidence.

Activity Sheet 3.11

Name: _____

A Letter

Use this sheet to plan a letter to someone you do not know well.

Name and address of the person to whom you are writing ↓

Your address →

_____

_____

_____

_____

Dear _____ ← **The person's name**

Today's date ↑

_____

_____ ← **Explain why you are writing to him or her.**

_____

_____

_____ ← **Write the information.**

_____

_____ ← **Write polite wishes.**

Sign off. → _____

_____ ← **Write your name.**

Teacher's notes
Supports Unit 19 of Pupil's Book 3. Help the children to write their home or school address correctly, including the postcode. Ensure that they know how to write the date, and the title and family name of the person to whom they are writing. The opening sentence should introduce the topic, so that the reader knows what the letter is about, and the final sentence should express polite wishes, for instance: *I hope this helps.*

Key to Writing Teacher's Book 2. Text © Christine Moorcroft and Les Ray 2003.
Illustrations © Letts Educational 2003. Published by Letts Educational 2003

Activity Sheet 3.12

Name: _____

Old News

Use this sheet to plan a newspaper article about an event in history.

Name of newspaper		Date

Headline

by _____

Subheading

Picture

Caption

Teacher's notes
Supports Unit 20 of Pupil's Book 3. Encourage the children to have fun thinking up a title for a newspaper which is appropriate for the period of history. The headline should summarise the events and it could be humorous. The article should begin by orientating the reader (giving background information) before telling the story. It should end by indicating what might happen next.

Key to Writing Teacher's Book 2. Text © Christine Moorcroft and Les Ray 2003.
Illustrations © Letts Educational 2003. Published by Letts Educational 2003

Activity Sheet 3.13

Name: _____

Shape It!

Use this sheet to write a shape poem about a fire.

Fire!

Teacher's notes
Supports Unit 23 of Pupil's Book 3. This sheet provides a format on which the children can write individual words, or sets of words, about a fire. They could write them in any direction which helps to create the effect they want.

Key to Writing Teacher's Book 2. Text © Christine Moorcroft and Les Ray 2003.
Illustrations © Letts Educational 2003. Published by Letts Educational 2003

Activity Sheet 3.14

Name: _____

Fast Food

Use this sheet to write new verses for the fast food poem.

Chorus

Chorus

Tomato sauce

Sausage roll

Chorus

Chorus

Teacher's notes
Supports Unit 24 of Pupil's Book 3. This sheet provides a format on which the children can write rhyming couplets to add to the fast food poem. Encourage them to try out ideas orally with a partner and then to write them on the sheet.

Key to Writing Teacher's Book 2. Text © Christine Moorcroft and Les Ray 2003.
Illustrations © Letts Educational 2003. Published by Letts Educational 2003

Activity Sheet 3.15

Name: _____

Gunerania's Wedding Cake

The king he baked a wedding cake upon a sunny day,
The king he baked a wedding cake, it was in the month of May,
The king he baked a wedding cake, he filled it with old clocks,
A cabbage, and an octopus, some apples and red socks.
He mixed it, he whisked it, he threw it on the floor,
He crushed it, he mushed it, and it slithered out the door.

- **Write a new verse for the poem.**

The king he baked a wedding cake _____
_____ ,

The king he baked a wedding cake _____
_____ ,

The king he baked a wedding cake _____
_____
_____ .

He _____ , he _____ , he _____ .
_____ ,
He _____ , he _____ , _____
_____ .

- **Write some notes for another verse.**

Teacher's notes
Supports Unit 26 of Pupil's Book 3. Read the verse on this sheet with the children and emphasise its lively rhythm. They should continue with the same rhythm as they add rhyming sections. Encourage them to think of ideas which are as silly as possible as long as they rhyme.

Key to Writing Teacher's Book 2. Text © Christine Moorcroft and Les Ray 2003.
Illustrations © Letts Educational 2003. Published by Letts Educational 2003

Activity Sheet 3.16

Name: _____

Create an Effect

- **Think of words to help you to create an exciting effect.**

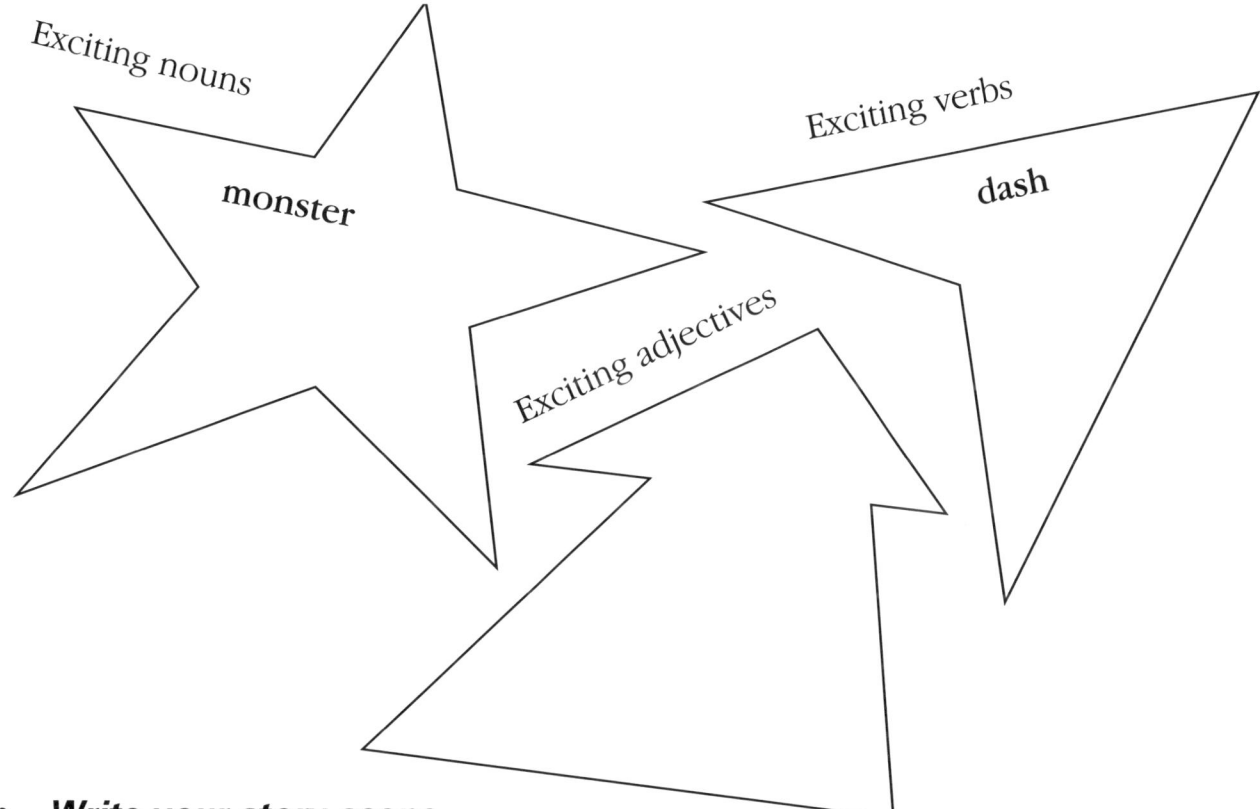

Exciting nouns

monster

Exciting verbs

dash

Exciting adjectives

- **Write your story scene.**

_____
_____
_____
_____
_____
_____
_____

Teacher's notes
Supports Unit 28 of Pupil's Book 3. The shapes in which the children write the words should help to create a feeling of excitement. Encourage them to write quickly (in order to create a lively flow of words) and then to use a thesaurus to find synonyms.

Key to Writing Teacher's Book 2. Text © Christine Moorcroft and Les Ray 2003.
Illustrations © Letts Educational 2003. Published by Letts Educational 2003

Target Statements for Writing

YEAR 4
As for Year 3 and:

Spelling	• Attempt to spell unfamiliar words using known conventions and rules and a range of strategies, including phonemic, morphemic and etymological. • Spell words for Y4 in Appendix List 2 in the NLS *Framework*. • Distinguish the spelling of common homophones, e.g. *hear* and *here*. • Use the dictionary to check spelling of words. • Use the apostrophe for omission.	WORD
Handwriting	• Use fluent joined handwriting for all writing except where other special forms are required.	
Style: language effects	• Use adjectives and adverbs selectively to create variety and add interest. • Use powerful verbs to show character or add impact. • Use language precisely and selectively in relation to text types, for instance to persuade or to convey information.	SENTENCE
Style: sentence construction	• Write simple and compound sentences and begin to use relative clauses. • Vary sentences showing characteristics of chosen form, adding phrases to enhance meaning.	
Punctuation	• Demarcate at least half of a written composition correctly, using the Y3 range of punctuation marks. • Begin to use the apostrophe for possession. • Use commas to separate phrases and clauses within sentences. • Use punctuation effectively in a range of text-types.	
Purpose and organisation	• Maintain consistent person and tense. • Use main features of story structure to organise events, varying openings, build-ups, conflicts and endings. • Use setting and characterisation to engage reader's interest, such as using the weather to create atmosphere. • In non-fiction, use basic features of text-types, such as introductory statements, followed by clear points leading to a conclusion. • Use paragraphs to structure narrative, for instance isolating an initiating event or introduction. Use appropriate layout conventions for non-fiction. • Show imagination through use of detail (e.g. to describe setting, build tension or show character's feelings or motives), creating interest, humour or suspense. • In non-fiction, attempt to interest, instruct, persuade or amuse the reader.	TEXT
Process	• Use different ways to plan writing, e.g. notes, diagrams, etc. • Mentally rehearse writing and re-read as a matter of habit. • Edit in relation to audience and purpose, enhancing or deleting, justifying choices.	

© Crown copyright 2000

Book 4

Summary of NLS objectives covered in *Key to Writing Book 4*

Unit	Theme	NLS objectives covered
1 Fire!	Fiction: Building Settings	• To investigate how settings are built up from small details and how the reader responds to them. • To understand how writers create imaginary worlds. • To develop use of settings, making use of adjectives.
2 I'm Scared!	Fiction: Building Settings	• To investigate how settings are built up from small details and how the reader responds to them. • To understand how settings influence events and incidents. • To develop use of settings making use of adjectives.
3 The Big Friendly Giant	Fiction: Likeable Characters	• To investigate how characters are built up from small details and how the reader responds to them. • To write character sketches focusing on small details to evoke sympathy. • To understand how the use of expressive language can describe attitudes and emotions.
4 Miss Slighcarp	Fiction: Nasty Characters	• To investigate how characters are built up from small details and how the reader responds to them. • To write character sketches focusing on small details to evoke dislike. • To understand how the use of expressive language can describe attitudes and emotions. • To write independently, linking own experience to situations in historical stories.
5 The Old Steam Train	Fiction: Chronology	• To explore chronology in narrative, using written or media texts. • To explore narrative order.
6 An Indian Folk Tale	Fiction: How Time Passes in Stories	• To explore chronology in narrative, using written or media texts. • To map out how much time passes in the course of a story.
7 When Alice Met Humpty Dumpty	Fiction: Playscripts	• To prepare, read and perform playscripts. • To chart the build-up of a play scene.
8 The Sun and the Wind	Fiction: Playscripts	• To prepare, read and perform playscripts. • To compare organisation of scripts with stories. • To write playscripts, using known stories as a basis.
9 The Wind	Fiction: Starting a Story	• To explore narrative order. • To plan a story, identifying the stages of its telling. • To use different ways of planning a story.
10 Annie's New Friend	Fiction: Building Up a Story	• To explore narrative order. • To plan a story, identifying the stages of its telling. • To explore main issues in a story about a dilemma.
11 The Sandcastle	Fiction: Climax and Conflict in a Story	• To explore narrative order. • To plan a story, identifying the stages of its telling. • To explore main issues in a story about a dilemma.
12 Rohan's Secret	Fiction: Resolution of a Story	• To explore narrative order. • To plan a story, identifying the stages of its telling. • To explore main issues in a story about a dilemma. • To write alternative endings.
13 Bedivere's Betrayal	Fiction: Historical Stories	• To write independently, linking own experience to situations in historical stories.

Book 4
Summary of NLS objectives (contd)

Unit	Theme	NLS objectives covered
14 Smith and the Blind Man	Fiction: Historical Stories	• To write independently, linking own experience to situations in historical stories, How would I have responded? What would I do next? • To identify social, moral or cultural issues in stories and write about how the characters would deal with them. • To explore main issues in a story about a dilemma.
15 Life in a Workhouse School	Non-fiction: Fact and Opinion	• To understand the terms *fact* and *opinion*. • To identify social, moral or cultural issues in stories. • To look at features of persuasive writing used to convince the reader. • To assemble and sequence points to present a point of view. • To present a point of view in writing.
16 A Leisure Survey	Non-fiction: Reports	• To identify different kinds of text: their content, structure, vocabulary, style, layout, purpose. • To identify features of non-fiction texts in print and IT, organisational devices and layout.
17 Silly News Weekly	Non-fiction: Newspaper Articles	• To identify different kinds of text: their content, structure, vocabulary, style, layout, purpose. • To identify the main features of newspapers. • To write newspaper-style reports.
18 Quick Truffles	Non-fiction: Instructions	• To identify different kinds of text: their content, structure, vocabulary, style, layout, purpose. • To identify the features of an instructional text. • To write clear instructions using conventions learned from reading.
19 A Trip to the Zoo	Non-fiction: Instructions	• To identify different kinds of text: their content, structure, vocabulary, style, layout, purpose. • To identify the features of an instructional text. • To write clear instructions using conventions learned from reading.
20 How To Fly a Hot Air Balloon	Non-fiction: Explanations	• To identify different kinds of text: their content, structure, vocabulary, style, layout, purpose. • To identify the key features of explanatory texts.
21 The Wild West	Non-fiction: Organisational Devices	• To identify features of non-fiction texts in print and IT, organisational devices and layout. • To improve the cohesion of written work through the use of organisational devices.
22 London	Non-fiction: Non-chronological Reports	• To identify different kinds of text: their content, structure, vocabulary, style, layout, purpose. • To write non-chronological reports, including the use of organisational devices.
23 Children's Games	Poetry: Imagination	• To write poems based on personal or imagined experience. • To understand the use of figurative language in poetry. • To write poems based on the structure and style of poems read. • To clap out and count the syllables in each line of regular poetry. • To recognise simple forms of poetry and their uses. • To write poems experimenting with different styles and structures. • To produce polished poetry through revision.

Summary of NLS objectives (contd)

Unit	Theme	NLS objectives covered
24 Limericks	Poetry: Pattern and Rhyme	• To write poems based on personal or imagined experience. • To identify patterns of rhyme or verse in poetry. • To write poems based on the structure and style of poems read. • To understand technical terms in poetry, for example: rhyme and rhythm. • To recognise simple forms of poetry and their uses. • To write poems experimenting with different styles and structures. • To produce polished poetry through revision.
25 The Poplar Field	Poetry: Verb Tenses	• To explore chronology in narrative, using written or media texts. • To understand the use of figurative language in poetry. • To identify clues which suggest poems are older. • To write poems based on the structure and style of poems read. • To write poems experimenting with different styles and structures.
26 High	Poetry: Action Verbs	• To experiment with powerful and expressive verbs. • To write poems experimenting with different styles and structures.
27 The History of Ice-Skating	Other Skills: Paragraphs	• To use paragraphs in writing to organise and sequence the narrative. • To identify how and why paragraphs are used to organise and sequence information. • To improve the cohesion of written explanations through paragraphing and organisational devices. • To understand how paragraphs or chapters are used to collect, order and build up ideas.
28 Life in the Second World War	Other Skills: Note-making	• To edit down passages, deleting the less important elements. • To scan texts to locate key words or phrases. • To mark extracts by annotating and by selecting key headings or words. • To make short notes. • To fill out brief notes into connected prose. • To summarise, in writing, key ideas from a paragraph.
29 Letters	Other Skills: Point of View	• To identify different kinds of text: their content, structure, vocabulary, style, layout, purpose. • To evaluate examples of arguments and discussions. • To consider how arguments are presented. • To look at features of persuasive writing used to convince the reader. • To assemble and sequence points to present a point of view. • To present a point of view in writing, for example: a letter.
30 Survive at School	Other Skills: Advertising	• To identify different kinds of text: their content, structure, vocabulary, style, layout, purpose. • To prepare for factual research. • To look at features of persuasive writing used to convince the reader. • To evaluate advertisements and their impact. • To design an advertisement, making use of features learnt by reading examples.

Book 4 Teacher's Notes

1 Fire!

Fiction: Building Settings

Objectives: To investigate how settings are built up from small details and how the reader responds to them. To understand how writers create imaginary worlds. To develop use of settings, making use of adjectives.

See also Activity Sheet 4.1

Starting the lesson: Read the passage with the children, communicating some of the excitement of the description. Much of the enthusiasm comes from the choice of effective verbs. They are lively and create images in the mind, for example: *belching*. Small details make the description more real. The smoke does not just come from the chimney — it comes from the cracks in it. Encourage the children to note down tiny details to use in their writing.

Activity Sheet 4.1 helps them to plan their letter about a bonfire. They will need to do some research about the festival they choose so they can include some interesting facts in their letters.

Sentence and word level: Look at what happens to words ending in *-e* when a vowel suffix such as *-ing* is added, for example: *dance/dancing*. List other words and any exceptions.

Discuss what happens when the word ends in *-y*: *empty/emptying*.

Consider the use of strong, accurate verbs, for example: *shot*, *gushing*. Encourage the children to use a thesaurus.

Plenary session: Use this session for monitoring and assessment. Bring the group together and invite the children to read their letters aloud. Ask other children to comment on the effectiveness of the descriptions of the bonfires. Can they suggest any different words which might improve the description? Discuss how the choice of one particular detail affects other details.

2 I'm Scared!

Fiction: Building Settings

Objectives: To investigate how settings are built up from small details and how the reader responds to them. To understand how settings influence events and incidents. To develop use of settings making use of adjectives.

See also Activity Sheet 4.2

Starting the lesson: Discuss with the children what makes a scary place. Is it the features of the place itself or the expectations in the mind? In the passage, the sense of the children being afraid is created by the inclusion of some details and also by the reactions of the children. Note how Nick says things and the way he reacts. This builds up a sense of the place not being pleasant.

Activity Sheet 4.2 helps them to plan their description of a haunted house.

Sentence and word level: Revise the punctuation of speech and the use of quotation marks.

Discuss how the author's description of the words, i.e. not just using *said*, can influence how the reader reacts.

Note how unstressed letters can cause problems with the spelling of a word, for example: *surprised*. List other words.

Extend this to the use of silent letters in words, for example: *whispered*.

Plenary session: Encourage the children to draft and edit their descriptions of the haunted house. They could use a thesaurus to find different adjectives. Revise how adjectives can be used to describe things and also to reveal feelings. Note any areas which need further work for individuals or for the class as a whole.

3 The Big Friendly Giant

Fiction: Likeable Characters

Objectives: To investigate how characters are built up from small details and how the reader responds to them. To write character sketches focusing on small details to evoke sympathy. To understand how the use of expressive language can describe attitudes and emotions.

Starting the lesson: Discuss with the children their expectation of a giant — and one who has kidnapped a little girl. Does the giant in the passage live up to their expectations — if not, why not? Note that it is his speech patterns and reactions which make us laugh at him and feel sorry for him. We cannot dislike him.

Sentence and word level: List the words which the giant mispronounces. Write the correct versions of the words and discuss their spellings.

Look at how the writer does not have to name the speakers towards the end of the passage because we can tell who is speaking. How? Revise the principle of new speaker–new line.

Plenary session: Invite the children to read their stories to the rest of the class. Ask other children to comment on what was effective and whether the aim of the writing has been achieved. Are the characters likeable? Which adjectives were used to create these effects?

Extend this work to look at other interpretations of giants in fiction and how they are portrayed.

4 Miss Slighcarp

Fiction: Nasty Characters

Objectives: To investigate how characters are built up from small details and how the reader responds to them. To write character sketches focusing on small details to evoke dislike. To understand how the use of expressive language can describe attitudes and emotions. To write independently, linking own experience to situations in historical stories.

See also Activity Sheet 4.3

Starting the lesson: It is very easy to dislike Miss Slighcarp. She fits into the stereotype of the evil teacher — almost in the manner of a fairy tale where the children are without their parents. Discuss with the children how *what* she says to the children, as well as *how* she says it, make us dislike her. Her actions are also cruel.

Activity Sheet 4.3 helps them to plan their character sketch of an aunt who becomes nasty. They should think about the aunt's actions and speech rather than description.

Sentence and word level: List any words which show that this story takes place in the historical past.

Encourage the use of a dictionary to find the meanings of the difficult words in the passage.

Revise the use of the possessive apostrophe, for example: *Miss Slighcarp's wrists*.

Consider the adverbs used in the passage to create the atmosphere.

Plenary session: Use the session to read the children's character sketches and discuss what they found difficult and easy. Ask the other children if the characters described really do seem to be nasty from what they say and do. Can they suggest any improvements? Encourage the children to look carefully at writing and punctuating sentences correctly.

5 The Old Steam Train

Fiction: Chronology

Objectives: To explore chronology in narrative, using written or media texts. To explore narrative order.

Starting the lesson: Remind the children that these pages are from a story written for very young children. Discuss some of the difficulties young children would have with reading a story.

Talk about how much information the pictures give you without having to use words. Ask the children to provide the necessary sentences.

Look closely at the chronology. How do we know the pictures are in the right order?

Sentence and word level: Revise the writing of simple sentences, especially when used for young children's literature.

When dealing with chronology, look at tenses of verbs (for example, *today I …, in the future I shall …*) and discuss any differences in the forms used for verb tenses.

Brainstorm more words ending in *-tion* (*station*). What other suffixes make this sound?

Plenary session: Use the pictures from the children's book to restructure the stories, for example: what happens if there is a flashback? Can we start at the end of the story and work backwards? Ask the children to comment on the work of others and how the ways in which you use time in a story can affect the narration.

6 An Indian Folk Tale

Fiction: How Time Passes in Stories

Objectives: To explore chronology in narrative, using written or media texts. To map out how much time passes in the course of a story.

See also Activity Sheet 4.4

Starting the lesson: Remind the children that the favourite opening sentence is *Once upon a time*, which sets a story at the beginning of a time structure. Time makes it easier for us to see how a story progresses.

Ask the children to work out the time sequence in this story: the girl grows up — at sixteen she gets married — more time moves on.

Discuss other stories where time is used differently.

Activity Sheet 4.4 helps them to continue the folk tale. They should introduce each paragraph with information about how time has passed. They could consider how the wives might react, whether the sister has changed since her marriage, what the climax of the story could be and how it could end.

Sentence and word level: Consider how the past tense is used to describe time in the past. Pick out examples in the passage of past tense verbs and change them to the present and the future tenses. Discuss any changes in the verb forms.

Remind the children that words such as *beautiful* come from other languages — *beau* is French for beautiful.

Plenary session: Encourage the children to redraft and edit their folk tales after they have read them to the class. It is important for them to realise that the piece they produce is not necessarily the finished item and that they can always improve their work in the light of comment. Note any areas which need further work for individuals or for the class as a whole.

Book 4 Teacher's Notes

7 When Alice Met Humpty Dumpty

Fiction: Playscripts

Objectives: To prepare, read and perform playscripts. To chart the build-up of a play scene.

See also Activity Sheet 4.5

Starting the lesson: Discuss the fact that a play is meant to be *watched* rather than read. Ask the children to point out how the format of a play is different from that of a traditional story. They should note that many of the words are not intended to be spoken — they are directions (*stage directions*) to the actor to show him or her how to create character through the way in which the words are spoken or by the movements to be made.

Activity Sheet 4.5 helps the children to write a playscript based on a well-known fairy story. Introduce and explain the term *cast list*.

Sentence and word level: Point out difficulties with words containing letters not usually pronounced, for example: *recognised*, *surprised*. Discuss strategies for learning how to spell these words, for example: pronouncing every syllable.

Revise the punctuation of speech and the conventions which go with it by changing the playscript into a conversation. The children will have to incorporate much of the stage direction into the dialogue.

Plenary session: Use this session for monitoring and assessment. Invite the children to act out their plays and ask other groups of children to be the directors. Suggest ways of saying the lines and of moving which are not included in the stage directions. Discuss which would be useful to include. Note any areas which need further work for individuals or for the class as a whole.

8 The Sun and the Wind

Fiction: Playscripts

Objectives: To prepare, read and perform playscripts. To compare organisation of scripts with stories. To write playscripts, using known stories as a basis.

See also Activity Sheet 4.5

Starting the lesson: Talk about the fables the children know. If they do not know any well-known Aesop stories, read some to them. Discuss the idea that such stories were written to teach people — hence the moral at the end.

Outline what setting instructions and stage directions are needed in order to change the passage into a play. Activity Sheet 4.5 helps the children to write a playscript based on a fable.

Sentence and word level: Investigate what happens to the root of a word when a suffix is added, for example: *argue/argument*, *power/powerful*. Encourage the children to develop rules and strategies to spell such words.

Consider why short paragraphs have been used in this kind of story. Why did the author not write much more and add more description?

Plenary session: Revise what the children have learned about playscripts and their features. Ask them to act out scenes from the playscript they have written and for others to ask what is happening or what they are trying to achieve. This will show the need for good stage directions and characterisation through dialogue.

9 The Wind

Fiction: Starting a Story

Objectives: To explore narrative order. To plan a story, identifying the stages of its telling. To use different ways of planning a story.

See also Activity Sheet 4.6

Starting the lesson: Discuss the notes on page 20 of the Pupil's Book. What different ways of making notes are shown? What sorts of ideas come to mind? The important principle is that the children should understand that brainstorming is a necessary *first stage* of writing, and that writing is not a one-stage process. Encourage the children to discuss the differences between the notes and the first draft.

Activity Sheet 4.6 helps them to set the scene of a story by describing the weather.

Sentence and word level: Look at the notes and the first draft. Point out the need for verbs and subjects and objects in writing simple sentences.

Think about different ways of starting sentences rather than *The …*.

Investigate the addition of the *-ing* suffix to verbs, particularly those ending in *e*. Outline reasons for dropping the *e*.

Plenary session: Use this session for monitoring and assessment. Planning should not be seen as an onerous task but as an important first step in communicating to the reader. Encourage the children to share their plans and first drafts with one another and to discuss possible improvements. They should then edit and redraft their work. List what they have learned and display it in class.

10 Annie's New Friend
Fiction: Building Up a Story

Objectives: To explore narrative order. To plan a story, identifying the stages of its telling. To explore main issues in a story about a dilemma.

See also Activity Sheet 4.7

Starting the lesson: Discuss the traditional format of a story: beginning, middle and end. Also talk about the importance of building up from a situation. Ask the children to think of well-known stories such as fairy tales which illustrate this. What is the situation? What happens to build this up? How is it resolved? Discuss some of the options after reading this passage. Does the character really exist?

Activity Sheet 4.7 helps them to write their stories about the huge, pink rabbit which only they can see. They could consider what happens when they talk to the rabbit. What will other people see? How will other people react? Encourage them to think of a surprise ending. Explain the term *resolution* (see Unit 12).

Sentence and word level: Brainstorm the different verbs which can be used instead of *said* in speech. Use a dictionary to find their meanings. Use a thesaurus to find alternatives.

Consider how the different verbs add something new to the description.

Investigate compound words in the passage, such as *playground* and *someone*. Can the children think of other examples?

Plenary session: Revise the stages of storytelling again. The children could discuss the steps they have used in their stories to build up to a moment of interest. Others could suggest improvements and the stories should be developed outside the session. What happens if all the children are given the same information? How many different stories can result?

11 The Sandcastle
Fiction: Climax and Conflict in a Story

Objectives: To explore narrative order. To plan a story, identifying the stages of its telling. To explore main issues in a story about a dilemma.

Starting the lesson: Discuss with the children what they can gather about the situation in the passage. Where are Biscuits and Tim? Why are they there? What is about to happen to them and why? You could discuss how far the children sympathise with the characters in the story — perhaps they have been in a similar bullying situation. Talk about the ways in which the story could be resolved. Will it have a happy or sad ending?

Sentence and word level: Take the example of *biscuits* as a commonly misspelled word. Use word derivation as a strategy: biscuits were originally baked twice in an oven to keep them fresh; hence the prefix *bis* (meaning *twice*) at the beginning. Find other examples where etymology can be used to help spelling.

Look at the use of shorter 'sentences' (*And much tougher too.*) to create tension, even though they are not grammatically correct.

Plenary session: Discuss with the children how conflict does not always have to mean violence! Analyse the children's stories to see how many kinds of conflict can be found. If some children still do not understand this concept, go back to well-known tales and fairy stories to identify the conflict and climax.

12 Rohan's Secret
Fiction: Resolution of a Story

Objectives: To explore narrative order. To plan a story, identifying the stages of its telling. To explore main issues in a story about a dilemma. To write alternative endings.

See also Activity Sheet 4.8

Starting the lesson: Revise with the children the idea of every story having a central idea which is developed into some kind of conflict or climax. Think of examples in fables or traditional tales. Discuss how stories need to be resolved for them to be satisfying to the reader. Revise the term *resolution*. Brainstorm examples of how stories end happily or unhappily and how they reach this point.

Activity Sheet 4.8 helps the children to plan their story about a magic object. They need to consider the resolution carefully, but also to plan the stages of the story which lead up to it.

Sentence and word level: Consider the spelling of past tenses of verbs: *bury/buried, draw/drew*. Find other examples.

Investigate the variety of sentence openings in the passage: *As he walked ..., Instead of ...*.

Consider examples of commonly misspelled words, for example: *stationery, practice*. Find strategies, such as mnemonics, to help to spell these words correctly in future.

Plenary session: Children often find it difficult to end their stories because they have not learned to plan their writing. Consider the endings to their stories — how many different kinds of endings are there? Did anyone die? Was it all a dream? Did it all end 'happily ever after'? Discuss which are the most convincing endings and which are simple, easy ways out.

Book 4 Teacher's Notes

13 Bedivere's Betrayal

Fiction: Historical Stories

Objective: To write independently, linking own experience to situations in historical stories.

Starting the lesson: Talk about how the children can confirm that this passage is set in a past time: situation, language or other details? Ask them why people should choose to write a story set in an historical past and whether they enjoy such stories. If not, why not? Can history teach us lessons about our own time? If so, how? Are the situations and problems the same as ours?

Sentence and word level: Investigate words containing a silent letter, for example: *knights*, *sword*. Find other examples and develop rules about silent letters in words.

Find words in the passage which we rarely use today, for example: *yonder*.

Consider the use of short, simple sentences to open stories. Look at how simple sentences can be made more complex by joining them with words such as *and*.

Plenary session: Use this session for monitoring and assessment. Bring the group together and invite the children to read their stories to the class. Ask other children to comment on whether the aim of the writing has been achieved in terms of historical accuracy. How far have they convinced their readers about the characters and the historical period?

14 Smith and the Blind Man

Fiction: Historical Stories

Objectives: To write independently, linking own experience to situations in historical stories. How would I have responded? What would I do next? To identify social, moral or cultural issues in stories and write about how the characters would deal with them. To explore main issues in a story about a dilemma.

See also Activity Sheet 4.9

Starting the lesson: Talk about the historical background to the passage so that the children can understand the moral dilemmas of the time: child poverty, children living without their parents, crime on the streets (Smith is a pickpocket), children drinking (*the gin's tempest*). This may change the children's perception about the characters and what they would have done.

Activity Sheet 4.9 helps them to plan their writing about meeting Smith. They should end by writing about what they would have done if they were Smith meeting the blind man. How would the story end then?

Sentence and word level: Identify any slang in the passage. Discuss standard English and when words become a part of acceptable usage. Which words are slang today, for example: *wicked*? How have these words changed their meaning?

Revise apostrophes for possession (*pity's sake*) and for omission (*I'm blind*). Find other examples.

Plenary session: You could link this work with PHSE and the whole idea of moral dilemmas. Always encourage the children to give reasons for their actions. If they are in roles, as in the writing exercise, they should be able to point to clues to these reasons in the writing.

15 Life in a Workhouse School

Non-fiction: Fact and Opinion

Objectives: To understand the terms *fact* and *opinion*. To identify social, moral or cultural issues in stories. To look at features of persuasive writing used to convince the reader. To assemble and sequence points to present a point of view. To present a point of view in writing.

Starting the lesson: Children often find it difficult to distinguish between fact and opinion; this affects their non-fiction writing. Read passage A and ask the children which points they can check, and how, for example: in an encyclopedia or in historical records. These points would be facts. In passage B, much is the opinion or feelings of the writer and cannot be checked, so should be treated with caution.

Sentence and word level: Investigate the plurals of words. How many rules can the children devise to help them with forming plurals? Is *children* a regular plural? Can they find any more like this?

Use a dictionary to find the meanings of abbreviations such as *a.m.*

Look closely at the tenses of the verbs used (for example: *could not*, *would be*) as opposed to the past tense in *were*. How do these affect the writer's meaning?

Plenary session: Non-fiction texts are always more difficult than fiction texts in their concepts, ideas and level of reading difficulty. However, it is vital that the children realise that all they read is not necessarily true or accurate. Invite the children to read their work and encourage others to ask the questions, *Can I prove this? Can it be tested?*

Book 4 Teacher's Notes

16 A Leisure Survey

Non-fiction: Reports

Objectives: To identify different kinds of text: their content, structure, vocabulary, style, layout, purpose.
To identify features of non-fiction texts in print and IT, organisational devices and layout.

Starting the lesson: Discuss with the children why they write reports — they organise factual information. They should be systematic and easy to read. Identify the use of the present tense for reports and how groups are generalised. It is not the job of a report to be personal. Hence the use of personal pronouns such as *I* and *we* is not appropriate.

Sentence and word level: Point out words in which unpronounced vowels can cause a spelling problem, for example: *interesting*, *Saturday*. Think of strategies for spelling such words, for example: sounding out all syllables.
Identify the present tense verbs. Change these to the past tense and discuss the effect of this on the report.

Plenary session: The children should now be able to identify the features of simple reports. Ask them to point out features from the passage or from their own reports. Encourage them to draft and edit their writing. Note any areas which need further work for individuals or for the class as a whole.

17 Silly News Weekly

Non-fiction: Newspaper Articles

Objectives: To identify different kinds of text: their content, structure, vocabulary, style, layout, purpose.
To identify the main features of newspapers. To write newspaper-style reports.
See also Activity Sheet 4.10

Starting the lesson: The children can have fun with the passage but it also contains all the features of a news article. Look at the use of a headline and the way in which subheadings focus on key issues and break up the writing. The first sentence sums up the story. The second develops the details. As the story develops in the past tense, the writer interviews others to give reported speech and quotations.
Activity Sheet 4.10 helps the children to plan their own silly news stories. Remind them to ask the questions, Who?

What? When? Where? How? Why? Revise the use of direct quotes and reported speech in news articles to give people's opinions.

Sentence and word level: Consider the use of hyphens in compound words such as *inner-city*. Discuss the use of hyphens and dashes. Hyphens join — dashes separate.
Make a list of all the features of a newspaper article and think of other examples for each of the grammatical features highlighted, for example: past tense, quotation, paragraphs.

Plenary session: Read the children's silly newspaper reports and ask them to identify the features of this genre from the passage or from their own writing. Look at more serious newspaper reports to prove that similar stylistic features appear in them too. Remind the children about how they are structured and use a particular sort of language. Can they think of any other genres which have similar features?

18 Quick Truffles

Non-fiction: Instructions

Objectives: To identify different kinds of text: their content, structure, vocabulary, style, layout, purpose.
To identify the features of an instructional text. To write clear instructions using conventions learned from reading.
See also Activity Sheet 4.11

Starting the lesson: Discuss with the children the features of a good set of instructions, as in a recipe. They have to be easy to understand or the recipe will be a failure. They should have a title and a list of what you will need. They should be written in steps — in the correct order. Verbs should be in the imperative (command) form. Ask the children to think of other kinds of instructions, for example: how to find their way somewhere. Do they have the same features?

Activity Sheet 4.11 helps them to plan their game and instructions.

Sentence and word level: Look at the derivation of words such as *chocolate*. The word originally comes from South America and came into English from travellers in the sixteenth century. Research other, similar words.
Identify the verbs in the imperative. Change them into another voice and tense and see how the use of a pronoun is needed. Discuss the effect of this.

Plenary session: Invite the children to read their instructions for a game to the class. The game could be posted on the school website.
Revise with them the features of instructions. Look at the structure of their instructions as well as the language and style. Test out simple instructions by asking the children to describe how to draw something simple, with a partner trying to do this. How good were they? What was missing?

43

Book 4 Teacher's Notes

19 A Trip to the Zoo
Non-fiction: Instructions

Objectives: To identify different kinds of text: their content, structure, vocabulary, style, layout, purpose. To identify the features of an instructional text. To write clear instructions using conventions learned from reading.

See also Activity Sheet 4.12

Starting the lesson: Discuss with the children the features of a good set of instructions to find their way to a place. They have to be easy to understand or they will get lost. Instructions should be written in steps — in the correct order. Verbs should be in the imperative (command) form. Ask the children to think of other kinds of instructions (for example, a recipe or how to play a game). Do they have the same stylistic features?

Activity Sheet 4.12 helps the children to decide what to include in their instructions to find the school. More than one set of instructions may be necessary, depending on the form of transport being used.

Sentence and word level: Consider the use of abbreviations in written instructions like this, for example: *St.* for *street*; *Rd.* for *road*. Brainstorm other abbreviations you could use.

Identify words which help in instructions, for example: *first ..., then ..., finally ...* . Discuss how these help the reader to move easily through the instructions, stage by stage. Discuss direction words, such as *second on the left*, *first on the right*.

Plenary session: The plenary should look at how good the instructions are. Can the reader follow them? What makes them easy or difficult to understand? Many children find it difficult to think of things in a series of steps in the correct order, so you could practise with sequencing exercises.

20 How to Fly a Hot Air Balloon
Non-fiction: Explanations

Objectives: To identify different kinds of text: their content, structure, vocabulary, style, layout, purpose. To identify the key features of explanatory texts.

Starting the lesson: Discuss the features of an explanation. An explanation should begin with a title summing up the topic. It should describe the parts of the thing to be explained and follow a clear sequence. The vocabulary can be technical but it should be explained. It is normally written in the present tense and uses action verbs (*connects*, *gets*, *puts*). It can often have an evaluation at the end.

Sentence and word level: Consider the kinds of words which help to sequence an explanation, for example: *after*, *first*, *then*.

Look carefully at the use of paragraphs. Is there a new paragraph each time the writer starts to talk about something else?

Discuss strategies to spell any technical words in the passage, for example: the Look, Cover, Say, Write, Check spelling strategy.

Plenary session: The aim of this session should be to revise the features of explanations and to ensure that the children can use them in their writing. Invite the children to read their explanations to the class. Ask others to comment on whether the aim of the writing has been achieved. What could be done to improve it? Encourage them to draft and edit their writing. The explanations could be posted on the school website

21 The Wild West
Non-fiction: Organisational Devices

Objectives: To identify features of non-fiction texts in print and IT, organisational devices and layout. To improve the cohesion of written work through the use of organisational devices.

Starting the lesson: Children often have to read and make notes from non-fiction books, the language of which is often much above their reading age. To help them, the book designer often uses devices to split the text and to make important points more recognisable. Identify in the passage: labelled diagrams, bullet points, boxed text, large titles, subheadings, italic fonts.

Sentence and word level: Consider how the same phoneme can make different sounds in words, for example: *thousands*, *journey*. Ask the children to find other examples. Devise strategies to spell these words.

Discuss how shortening a text (for example, by using bullet points) allows the writer to communicate the same idea but to avoid writing complex sentences.

Plenary session: Awareness of organisational devices is key to being able to deal with complex non-fiction texts. Computer technology allows writers and designers to use and manipulate these devices. Consider with the children what the writing would have been like without them. Would it be easier or more difficult to understand? Make a display of the information pages about Native Americans. Discuss whether the organisational devices have been used appropriately.

Book 4 Teacher's Notes

22 London
Non-fiction: Non-chronological Reports

Objectives: To identify different kinds of text: their content, structure, vocabulary, style, layout, purpose. To write non-chronological reports, including the use of organisational devices.

See also Activity Sheet 4.13

Starting the lesson: Reports are usually sequential to make the facts clear. However, they are sometimes written using a different structure. In this example, from geography, London is written about using a series of (unseen) headings: size, climate, industries. Such reports do not follow a time sequence and are therefore non-chronological.

Activity Sheet 4.13 helps them to plan a non-chronological report for a geography book.

Sentence and word level: Consider the use of capital letters for proper nouns: the name of the city, the river, the country. Ask the children to think of other examples. Identify other nouns in the passage and discuss why these do not have capital letters.

Take some of the simple sentences (for example, in the first paragraph) and make them into more complex sentences by adding conjunctions, such as *and*. Discuss the effect of this.

Plenary session: Often the simplest of writing can appear the most complicated, so encourage the children to read their non-chronological reports. Encourage them to draft and edit their writing.

Outline the features of this kind of report. You may wish to compare it to other kinds of reports. Note any areas which need further work for individuals or for the class as a whole.

23 Children's Games
Poetry: Imagination

Objectives: To write poems based on personal or imagined experience. To understand the use of figurative language in poetry. To write poems based on the structure and style of poems read. To clap out and count the syllables in each line of regular poetry. To recognise simple forms of poetry and their uses. To write poems experimenting with different styles and structures. To produce polished poetry through revision.

See also Activity Sheet 4.14

Starting the lesson: Discuss what the children see in the picture in the Pupil's Book, page 48. Explain that the games shown in the picture were played in the fifteenth century.

Outline the format of a haiku: seventeen syllables in all, following a five-seven-five pattern with no rhyme. The final line needs to contain a kind of surprise which makes the description seem new.

Activity Sheet 4.14 helps the children to write their own haiku.

Sentence and word level: Talk about how poems need not use complete sentences. Find examples. Identify what would be needed to make these into complete sentences. How can we understand the writer's meaning if he or she does not use sentences?

Discuss onomatopoeic words (where sound is linked with the sense of a word, as in *snicker-snacker*).

Plenary session: Haiku are tiny, complete poems which will enable all children to be successful at writing. Invite the children to read their haiku about a painting to the class. Ask other children to comment on what was effective. What could be done to improve them?

24 Limericks
Poetry: Pattern and Rhyme

Objectives: To write poems based on personal or imagined experience. To identify patterns of rhyme or verse in poetry. To write poems based on the structure and style of poems read. To understand technical terms in poetry, for example: rhyme and rhythm. To recognise simple forms of poetry and their uses. To write poems experimenting with different styles and structures. To produce polished poetry through revision.

Starting the lesson: Ask the children whether poems always have to rhyme. What does rhyme add to poetry? Discuss the format of a limerick: line lengths (beat out the syllables) and rhyme pattern (identify which lines rhyme). The poems are jokes and the last line makes the funny point. Read the poems and see how they match the pattern.

Sentence and word level: Look carefully at the rhymes and outline which phonemes make the same sounds, for example: as in *Peru* and *knew*. Ask the children to think of any other sounds these phonemes might make.

Talk about how poems do not need to be written in grammatically correct sentences.

Plenary session: Use this session for monitoring and assessment. Are there any children who cannot grasp the idea of rhyme? This is an important skill for phonological awareness, so it is vital the skill is taught. Others may have difficulty with rhythm.

Book 4 Teacher's Notes

25 The Poplar Field
Poetry: Verb Tenses

Objectives: To explore chronology in narrative, using written or media texts. To understand the use of figurative language in poetry. To identify clues which suggest poems are older. To write poems based on the structure and style of poems read. To write poems experimenting with different styles and structures.
See also Activity Sheet 4.15

Starting the lesson: Explain to the children that this poem was written more than 200 years ago and so some of the words may be difficult. Read the poem and identify the use of verb tenses in the various verses — it starts in the present because the poet is there by the river looking at where the trees were. He then moves to the past when the trees were there and to the future when he will be dead.
   Activity Sheet 4.15 helps them to plan their autobiography using the correct verb tenses.

Sentence and word level: Find examples of the three verb tenses in the poem. Experiment with changing them to other tenses to see the effect this has on the poem.
   List the rhyming words in the poem and note which sounds are made by which combinations of letters. Find other examples of words with the same combinations, making the same or different sounds.

Plenary session: The children's work on their autobiographies links closely with the sentence-level work. Analysis of the children's writing should make you aware of which children are finding verb tenses difficult. Encourage them to think of simple time zones (*today I ..., yesterday I ..., tomorrow I shall ...*) and to change the same piece of writing using different tenses accordingly.

26 High
Poetry: Action Verbs

Objectives: To experiment with powerful and expressive verbs. To write poems experimenting with different styles and structures.

Starting the lesson: Read the poem with the children and identify the verbs the poet uses. Encourage them to use a thesaurus to find different verbs with a similar meaning. Discuss whether these are as good as, or better than, the original verb. Writers choose verbs not just for meaning but also to suggest shades of meaning and associations — they create images in the mind; so the more exact the verb, the better.

Sentence and word level: Consider words like *wind* and discuss with the children how the same spelling can sound very different, for example: *wind in the kite, in the wind.* Think of other examples (*row, read*). Look at words containing the silent *h*, as in *whisper* and *whistle.* Find other examples.
   Find old-fashioned words in the passage which we no longer use. The children could look up their meanings in a dictionary.

Plenary session: After reading their poems about a bird to the class, the children could use a thesaurus to have a race. Ask them to 'find as many words of similar meaning for ...'. This will encourage them to think of words other than *got* or *went* when describing processes. They could substitute words in their writing, but must be prepared to say why one verb is better than the other in this context.

27 The History of Ice-Skating
Other Skills: Paragraphs

Objectives: To use paragraphs in writing to organise and sequence the narrative. To identify how and why paragraphs are used to organise and sequence information. To improve the cohesion of written explanations through paragraphing and organisational devices. To understand how paragraphs or chapters are used to collect, order and build up ideas.

Starting the lesson: Paragraphs are an essential structural element to all writing. The children need to be aware that writing should be divided into paragraphs to make it more easily understood. Each time a writer changes his or her subject, a new paragraph should be started. Each paragraph should have a topic sentence — one which can sum up the paragraph. All the other sentences should exemplify this point.

Sentence and word level: Revise what happens to root words when the vowel suffix *-ing* is added, for example: *skate/skating, tie/tying*. Think of other examples and devise some helpful strategies.
   Summarise each paragraph and find its topic sentence. List the sentences which reinforce the message of the topic sentence.

Plenary session: Use this session for monitoring and assessment of the use of paragraphs in the children's own sporting histories. Some of the children will find paragraphs difficult because they will not stop to think about whether they are changing subject or not. Encourage sequencing and editing. Note any areas which need further work for individuals or for the class as a whole.

Book 4 Teacher's Notes

28 Life in the Second World War

Other Skills: Note-making

Objectives: To edit down passages, deleting the less important elements. To scan texts to locate key words or phrases. To mark extracts by annotating and by selecting key headings or words. To make short notes. To fill out brief notes into connected prose. To summarise, in writing, key ideas from a paragraph.

See also Activity Sheet 4.16

Starting the lesson: Children are often asked to make notes, particularly from non-fiction texts where technical language can be difficult. Discuss different ways to make notes, for example: numbered lists, charts, spider diagrams. Model these with the class.

Activity Sheet 4.16 helps them with the questions in section **b**, on page 59 of the Pupil's Book.

Sentence and word level: Consider some of the words in the passage specific to history (for example, *government*, *designed*, *ration*), all of which are difficult to spell. Look for strategies to help with the spelling, for example: mnemonics — ***Govern* is in *government***.

Discuss organisational devices used in non-fiction — bullet points, fonts, and so on (see Unit 21).

Plenary session: Discuss with the children which kind of note-making they find easy or difficult — and why. Practise with them how to scan and mark texts in order to extract information. Encourage them to use their own words as far as possible.

29 Letters

Other Skills: Point of View

Objectives: To identify different kinds of text: their content, structure, vocabulary, style, layout, purpose. To evaluate examples of arguments and discussions. To consider how arguments are presented. To look at features of persuasive writing used to convince the reader. To assemble and sequence points to present a point of view. To present a point of view in writing, for example: a letter.

See also Activity Sheet 4.17

Starting the lesson: Identify the features of letters, for example: address, opening greeting and ending. Discuss which are suitable for which audiences. For example, *Dear Sir ... Yours faithfully* is formal; *Dear Mr ... Yours sincerely* is less formal; but *Hi there ... All the best* is informal. When should they use each style?

Activity Sheet 4.17 provides a writing frame for a formal letter.

Sentence and word level: Consider how to set out an address on a letter and how abbreviations can be used.

List the words most used in letters (for example: *dear*, *sincerely*, *yours*) and develop strategies to spell them correctly.

Talk about how e-mails are both similar to and different from letters. Why are certain features of letters not needed in e-mails?

Plenary session: It helps if the children have used a computer to produce their letters. This facilitates editing. Invite them to read their letters to the class. What suggestions can the others make to improve them? Do they use the correct tone and style?

30 Survive at School

Other Skills: Advertising

Objectives: To identify different kinds of text: their content, structure, vocabulary, style, layout, purpose. To prepare for factual research. To look at features of persuasive writing used to convince the reader. To evaluate advertisements and their impact. To design an advertisement, making use of features learnt by reading examples.

Starting the lesson: Discuss which advertisements the children remember best: on TV, in the cinema, on billboards or in magazines. How are these different from other kinds of advertisements, for example: to sell a bicycle in the newspaper? Consider the purpose, and the effects the author wants to create. Discuss whether the advertisements on page 62 are successful.

Sentence and word level: List the words used most in advertisements, for example: *new*, *improved*. Find other words meaning the same in a thesaurus; discuss their effects.

Collect slogans used in advertising. Are they written in complete sentences? Do they use made-up words?

Plenary session: Invite the children to present their advertisements to the class. Ask the others to comment on what is effective, and why. Revise sentence-level work involving adjectives and superlatives.

Remind the children that the style of their writing will be influenced by its purpose and the intended audience.

Activity Sheet 4.1

Name: _____

Fire!

Use this sheet to plan your letter about a festival bonfire.

Name of the festival:
Interesting facts about the festival
Time of day of the bonfire:
The weather conditions:
How you feel about the scene

What does the festival celebrate? What else happens during the festival? Why is there a bonfire?

Words to describe the scene

Verbs		Adjectives	
To show action	To communicate sound	To show how you feel	To add colour
gushes	*spat*	*wonderful*	*orange*

Teacher's notes
Supports Unit 1 of Pupil's Book 4. Make lists of adjectives (shape, size, colour, texture) to give the children a starting point. Make sure they use a thesaurus to re-examine the verbs they use. Discuss with them how, if they choose one particular detail, such as time of day or weather, it will influence all the other detail.

Activity Sheet 4.2

Name: _____

The Haunted House

Use this sheet to plan your description of your visit to a haunted house.

What you know about the house which makes you feel afraid

Time of day or night

Sounds

> Does the front door creak? Do the bats flutter and squeak? Do branches tap on the windows?

Small details

> In the dark, what does a coat over a chair remind you of? What about shadows moving?

Useful adjectives

What you might say to persuade yourself that things are not as bad as they seem

Teacher's notes
Supports Unit 2 of Pupil's Book 4. The aim of the writing is for the children to choose adjectives which suggest their feelings — in this case negative ones. They could use a thesaurus to find a whole range of words. Encourage them to be selective — their original choice of words may not be used in the end. Discuss with them how the state of mind of the storyteller may also influence what he or she sees, hears and feels.

Key to Writing Teacher's Book 2. Text © Christine Moorcroft and Les Ray 2003.
Illustrations © Letts Educational 2003. Published by Letts Educational 2003

Activity Sheet 4.3

Name: _____

The Nasty Aunt

Use this sheet to make notes for a story about a kind aunt who becomes nasty when your parents go away.

Describe the aunt as a pleasant character when your parents are there.

What changes do you notice when they have gone?

Describe a situation which brings you into conflict with your aunt.

What happens to you?

Describe how you get your revenge on your aunt.

Think of a good ending to your story.

Teacher's notes
Supports Unit 4 of Pupil's Book 4. Model with the children how they can create a story structure like the one in the passage in the Pupil's Book. They should concentrate on how a character can be created by *what* he or she says and does and *how* he or she says or does it, as much as by how he or she looks. Encourage them not to concentrate too much on narrative.

Activity Sheet 4.4

Name: _____

An Indian Folk Tale

Use this sheet to continue the Indian folk tale.

Title:

Some details about the festival

What is it called? What happens?

Continue the folk tale. Remember to introduce each paragraph with information about how time has passed.

What happens to bring the story to a climax?

What happens to the brothers in the end?

Continue on the back of the sheet if necessary.

Teacher's notes
Supports Unit 6 of Pupil's Book 4. Folk or fairy tales from all cultures seem to have similar structures, story lines and characters because they were originally produced to entertain and teach a non-literate population. Look closely at the structures of other well-known tales with the children before they continue this story.

Key to Writing Teacher's Book 2. Text © Christine Moorcroft and Les Ray 2003.
Illustrations © Letts Educational 2003. Published by Letts Educational 2003

Activity Sheet 4.5

Name: _____

A Playscript

Use this sheet to write a playscript.

Title:
Cast list:
Stage directions to introduce the play:

Name of character	What he or she says

Continue on the back of the sheet.

Remember:
- Do not use speech marks.
- Put the name of the speakers on the left so that the actors know when to speak. Describe the speakers before they start.
- Show how a character feels or reacts in stage directions in brackets. An actor will not know how to say the lines or what kind of character you want.

Teacher's notes
Supports Units 7 and 8 of Pupil's Book 4. Model with the children how to structure and write the first few lines of dialogue. Discuss with them why the stylistic features are relevant, for example: stage directions to tell the actor how to behave, scene instructions to help the stage designer.

Activity Sheet 4.6

Name: _____

Brainstorming

- *Use this sheet to set the scene of a story using the weather.*

Title	Setting
Time of day	Weather

How will it affect all your senses?	
Sight	
Hearing	
Touch	
Taste	
Smell	

Useful strong verbs and adjectives	
Verbs	Adjectives

Comparisons to make the scene come alive

- *Write your first draft in your book or on the back of this sheet.*
- *Read it to a partner and ask for suggestions for improving it.*

Teacher's notes
Supports Unit 9 of Pupil's Book 4. Drafting a piece of work is vitally important in writing. Many children tend to think this is a waste of time because they know what they want to write, but few can keep their narrative going. Encourage them to plan and draft and not to be afraid to change their minds.

Key to Writing Teacher's Book 2. Text © Christine Moorcroft and Les Ray 2003.
Illustrations © Letts Educational 2003. Published by Letts Educational 2003

Activity Sheet 4.7

Name: _____

The Huge Pink Rabbit

Use this sheet to plan your story about the huge, pink, talking rabbit which only you can see.

Introduction

Think of a situation involving some characters, like the one in Annie's New Friend.

Build up the story

Use dialogue to show character and what happens.

Resolution (ending)

Teacher's notes
Supports Unit 10 of Pupil's Book 4. Model with the children a variety of ways through the story. Encourage them to realise that one small change early on can redirect the narrative. Characters are created by what they say and what they do, as well as how they look and how we react to them.

Activity Sheet 4.8

Name: _____

Doing Something Wrong

Use this sheet to plan a story in which you become really good at something after finding a magic object. Concentrate on the resolution of the story.

Title:
Introduction
Build up the story
Climax of the story
Resolution

What is the magic object? How does it help you to become good at something?

What excuses will you give? How much information can you give before you get caught out?

How does the teacher finally learn the truth?

Teacher's notes
Supports Unit 12 of Pupil's Book 4. This story structure revolves around a moral dilemma and so lends itself to much discussion among the children. Link it to PHSE. Encourage them to give their reasons why they would behave in a certain way.

Activity Sheet 4.9

Name: _____

Life in Victorian Times

Use this sheet to plan your writing about meeting Smith in Victorian times.

Do you go to school? Describe it.		
Do you have to work? Doing what?		
Write about how you meet Smith and become involved with his adventures.		
What Smith wears, what he eats and drinks, where he lives	What Smith says and the way he says it	Smith's attitudes towards life, which may be very different to your own
What would I have done?		

Teacher's notes
Supports Unit 14 of Pupil's Book 4. The children will probably have covered some of the historical topics in class, but this is an ideal opportunity to research. Encourage the children to use the library or the Internet and to revise their note-taking skills.

Activity Sheet 4.10

Name: _____

Silly News

Use this sheet to write an article about an unimportant event at school.

Headline

by _____

Subheading		Picture

	Caption

Subheading

Remember:
- Use the past tense.
- Do not use I and me.
- Do not give your own opinions.

Teacher's notes
Supports Unit 17 of Pupil's Book 4. Model with the children what the features of a newspaper article are and where they are to be found in the text in the Pupil's Book. Encourage them to write short, often silly, articles until they are clear about the style and the structure needed. For the final version, use a computer to produce a professional-looking newspaper article.

Key to Writing Teacher's Book 2. Text © Christine Moorcroft and Les Ray 2003.
Illustrations © Letts Educational 2003. Published by Letts Educational 2003

Activity Sheet 4.11

Name: _____

Instructions

Use this sheet to plan your instructions for a game.

Name of the game:
You need:
Aim of the game:
How to play the game: Step 1   Step 2   Step 3

End of the game	Diagram

Teacher's notes
Supports Unit 18 of Pupil's Book 4. Model with the children the features of instructions and where they are to be found in the passage in the Pupil's Book. Encourage them to use notes, numbered lists and diagrams to make their instructions clear. Test the instructions to see if they work. If not, change them!

Activity Sheet 4.12

Name: _____

How to Find …

Use this sheet to plan your instructions for finding your school.

How to find:	
From where?	
Map	Plan of school

Instructions

1

2

3

4

Teacher's notes
Supports Unit 19 of Pupil's Book 4. Model with the children the features of this kind of instructions and where they are to be found in the passage in the Pupil's Book. Encourage them to use notes, numbered lists, maps and plans to make their directions clear. Test the instructions to to see if they work. If not, how can they be improved?

Activity Sheet 4.13

Name: _____

A Non-chronological Report

Use this sheet to plan a report about a country for a geography book.

Country: _____

Topic headings:

Write notes about each heading, using facts. Use the present tense.

What is the land like — mountains? desert?

Location	Landscape features
Draw a map	
Size	Main rivers
Climate	Exports
Population	Problems

Teacher's notes
Supports Unit 22 of Pupil's Book 4. Model with the children the features of non-chronological reports and where these are to be found in the passage in the Pupil's Book. Encourage them to use notes, numbered lists, subheadings, diagrams and maps to make their reports clear.

Activity Sheet 4.14

Name: _____

Haiku

- **How many syllables are there in each line of a haiku?**

  Onward go the blind.　　　　Number of syllables in line 1: _____
  Very slowly as they walk.　　Number of syllables in line 2: _____
  All is a shadow　　　　　　Number of syllables in line 3: _____

- **Write three haiku about a painting you like.**

Name of painting:
Brainstorm ideas about what you think you would be able to hear, see, smell and feel if you were in the picture.

Remember to try for a surprise in line 3!

Use these syllable boxes to help you to write the haiku.

Line 1
Line 2
Line 3

Line 1
Line 2
Line 3

Line 1
Line 2
Line 3

Teacher's notes
Supports Unit 23 of Pupil's Book 4. Provide copies of a range of paintings so that the children can choose one as the subject for their haiku. Encourage them to count out syllables (this will link with word-level work) and to follow the pattern of the haiku.

Key to Writing Teacher's Book 2. Text © Christine Moorcroft and Les Ray 2003.
Illustrations © Letts Educational 2003. Published by Letts Educational 2003

Activity Sheet 4.15

Name: _____

My Autobiography

Use this sheet to plan your autobiography.

Important dates and events in your life so far
(Choose two important events and make notes on them.)

Which tense will you use?

Describe the kind of person you are today.

Describe what you want to do and the kind of person you want to be in the future.

Teacher's notes
Supports Unit 25 of Pupil's Book 4. Remember that the children cannot include everything about their lives in their brief autobiography, so encourage them to be selective and to write interestingly about a few events rather than list everything. Model with them how they can make one small event interesting to others.

Activity Sheet 4.16

Name: _____

Making Notes

Use this sheet to make notes about life in the Second World War from the passage in the Pupil's Book.

Numbers and lists

1 _____

2 _____

3 _____

4 _____

A spider diagram

- To share resources
- Government restrictions

A time-line

|————————————|————————————|————————————|

1940
Tower of London used to grow vegetables

1941

1942

A chart

Features of rationing	Advantages
Clothes rationing	No shortage of cloth — could not import

Teacher's notes
Supports Unit 28 of Pupil's Book 4. Model with the children how to make notes using each format. Discuss with them which is best for certain kinds of tasks. The important factor in making notes is that the children should write the final version in their own words and not copy out large parts of the original text.

Key to Writing Teacher's Book 2. Text © Christine Moorcroft and Les Ray 2003.
Illustrations © Letts Educational 2003. Published by Letts Educational 2003

Activity Sheet 4.17

Name: _____

A Formal Letter

Use this sheet to plan a formal letter.

Name and address of the person to whom you are writing

Your address

_____
_____
_____
_____

_____
_____
_____
_____

The date

Dear Sir or Madam

_____
_____
_____
_____
_____
_____
_____
_____

List your arguments and think of evidence to back up each one. Make these personal arguments (use I and we).

Be positive — offer suggestions to deal with the issue.

Yours faithfully

_____

Write your name.

Teacher's notes
Supports Unit 29 of Pupil's Book 4. Discuss with the children the importance of knowing their audience when writing and what their expectations might be about style and content. Model with them how a letter to a close friend may be very different in style and content to one written to their headteacher.